Better Teaching and Learning
in the Digital Classroom

Better Teaching and Learning in the Digital Classroom

Edited by David T. Gordon

HARVARD EDUCATION PRESS

Library of Congress Control Number: 2003110311

Library Edition: ISBN 1-891792-17-2
Paperback Edition: ISBN 1-891792-16-4

Published by Harvard Education Press,
an imprint of the Harvard Education Publishing Group

Harvard Education Press
8 Story Street
Cambridge, MA 02138

Cover design by Alyssa Morris
Cover photo by Ryan McVay © Getty Images

Contents

Better Teaching and Learning in the Digital Classroom

Introduction: Cassandra, Pollyanna, and All of Us in Between

By David T. Gordon

T he turn of the millennium is already starting to feel like a long
time ago. In 2000, when we published *The Digital Classroom:
How Technology Is Changing the Way We Teach and Learn*,
Bill Clinton was president, September 11 was still an unremarkable
date on the calendar, and "No Child Left Behind" was a slogan of lib-
eral education groups, not the moniker of a sweeping education bill
sponsored by a conservative president.

In that book, teachers, researchers, and reporters discussed the potential of powerful new technologies to transform K–12 teaching and
learning, just as they had transformed global business, science, communications, and, to some extent, higher education in the 1990s. At the
same time, a debate was simmering in education circles about whether
technology was a boondoggle or a boon to education, a debate that occasionally spilled over into the mainstream press. Critics warned, Cas-
sandra-like, that schools were being snookered by Big Business into
wasting tax dollars on technology products that were physically and de-

velopmentally dangerous to children and couldn't improve student outcomes, or both.

The mainstream press picked up the scent of conspiracy. In the fall of 2000, *U.S. News & World Report* splashed on its cover the scare-mongering headline, "Why Computers Fail as Teachers," as though the nation's youth had been turned over to the custody of corporate robots. Of course, computers had not failed at being teachers because they hadn't tried to be teachers—or hadn't been tried *as* teachers. Imagine the headline: "Why Pencils Fail as Teachers" or "What Notebooks Can't Teach Your Kids."

New technologies are, in many respects, far more powerful learning tools than books, pencils, paper, and chalk. But in many other ways they're no different, and without high-quality instruction delivered by caring, competent teachers, few students have a chance of succeeding, regardless of whether they have a Pentium 4 processor or a No. 2 pencil. The answer to the poor use of computers or incomplete research about their effect on educational outcomes is not to ignore the machines or banish them from the classroom.

Critics of technology have raised important points. They remind us that children deserve to have a rich variety of learning experiences, that the depth of the human relationships among students and teachers is as much a predictor of educational success as the power of their Intel processors, and that technology is no magic cure for struggling schools. They sound appropriate warnings that the high-tech industry should be cautious of making claims it can't fulfill, especially with our children's future at stake. They rightly call for more research into the effects of new technologies on learning. And on these points, enthusiasts of educational technology largely agree.

The challenge for 21st-century educators is to find balanced, sensible, and pedagogically sound ways of using these remarkable new tools. After all, these are tools that students will be expected to use in most careers and that they are already using in their everyday lives. Indeed, "new" technologies are really only new to those of us who grew up without them. To students raised in the past decade or two, these "innovations" are nothing of the kind: they are utterly commonplace means of communication, information gathering, and entertainment. The average adolescent (*screenagers* is one name for them) is more likely to carry a cell phone—which she can use to call home, calculate figures, play digital blackjack, surf the Web, and write memos—than she is to carry a pen and pad. And she is oblivious to the graying Cassandras' howls.

In *Better Teaching and Learning in the Digital Classroom*, which was developed as a companion to the earlier volume, the question of whether to move ahead with an infusion of new technologies in K–12 classrooms is not addressed since by now it is moot. The aim here is to explore the many ways educators can make the most of the technology that may already be available to them. The authors are not technology Pollyanas—technology's bells and whistles are not what interest them, but how to improve the work that goes on in real classrooms. They are well aware that K–12 schools have to succeed within the boundaries of state standards and accountability systems, with or without technology.

The book begins the basic question of what it means to teach and learn in this new age. In light of the ways mass media saturate young people with images, sounds, and texts that convey all kinds of messages and values, how can teachers, who may not be tech savvy, teach tech-savvy students to develop their critical thinking skills? Andrea Oseas and Julie M. Wood consider that puzzle in a discussion of what's called multiple literacies. In an environment marked by standardized curriculum and tests, Oseas and Wood write, suggesting that teachers take the time to focus on critical thinking skills may seem unnecessary or even unfair. But teaching students to question and weigh what they see, hear, and read in a 24/7 culture couldn't be more essential if they are to become independent, civic-minded adults—a point Oseas and Wood demonstrate with examples from real classrooms where such teaching is taking place.

Many of those global images and messages students receive are about other countries and cultures. Globalization, which is fueled by new technologies, has transformed not only the world but each small community. Through the Internet, Beijing is accessible to Biloxi, just as Levittown is reachable from Lithuania. The awful events of September 11, 2001, and the wars they have spawned, have given even more significance to international education. Two pioneers of using technology for global education, Kristi Rennebohm Franz and Edwin Gragert, discuss how students and teachers are connecting around the world via new technologies to learn more about one another's countries, share ideas and perspectives, and prepare students of all nations for citizenship in the world and the global challenges they'll face as adults.

Just as new technologies are helping people link up across continents, so too are they making it easier for children with special needs to connect with their classmates by working from the same curriculum. In a profile of work being done at the Center for Applied Special Technology (CAST) in Massachusetts, I present researchers with a bold vision of how digital text can be used to transform—or rescue, really—the K–12 experiences of millions of students with special needs. Students who otherwise would not be able to keep up with grade-level work because of learning or physical disabilities are now able to participate in the same learning activities as their peers because the software they use has been created to accommodate a wide variety of learning styles.

Digital technology is bringing parents, teachers, and students together, too. Master teacher Kristi Rennebohm Franz describes her use of classroom web pages where students post their work, showing that such innovations are creating new traditions in home-school relationships. Through "virtual" classroom visits via the Web, parents stay current with what's happening at school and follow their children's progress online. When parent-teacher-student conferences take place, there are no surprises—and much more informed discussions. This work is especially promising in light of research that shows the importance of getting parents involved in their children's education.

The use of handheld computers like Pocket PCs are also changing the look of traditional classrooms. Researchers Cathleen A. Norris and Elliot Soloway, who have studied the use of handhelds in more than 1,000 classrooms, find a number of benefits in using low-cost handheld computers. These include easier collaboration by students on group projects, writing and revision when students are away from desktops, the creation of digital portfolios of student work, and other basic classroom tasks.

Education technologist David Niguidula takes us inside schools that use digital portfolios to improve the process of student assessment, data collection and analysis, and faculty reflection on teaching and learning. He addresses the dilemmas of assessment in the context of demanding state-accountability systems, and he spells out the pluses and minuses of using computer-organized data for such purposes. With appropriate caveats, he demonstrates how technology can give educators fresh views of their own work and that of their students, all with the goal of improving classroom instruction.

Of course, the ease with which students can cut and paste text presents special challenges for those who want to foil plagiarism and teach good research habits. As Michael Sadowski demonstrates, literally hundreds of websites now offer prewritten or custom-written essays, a temptation to lazy, desperate, or confused students facing deadlines. But a number of other sites now offer valuable services to detect plagiarism—a case of using technology to cure one of the ills it spawns.

Drawing from his rich experience as an instructional designer and educator, James Moore discusses ways of creating educational web environments that are rich in content but easy-to-use, flexible, and adaptable to a teacher's particular goals and methods. As websites today offer more content and interactive features, such as streaming video, how can we ensure that these sites provide more than bells and whistles— that they offer direct benefits for teaching and learning? Moore offers clear suggestions and helpful examples of what can be done.

Some teachers are using online networks to beef up their credentials and get involved in professional communities, as one of my own articles describes. The proliferation of formal online courses is allowing many to further their education or complete required in-service training. Less formal sites give teachers a place to swap lesson plans and war stories in online "personal offices" and "conference rooms," where they can discuss the subject they teach or particular professional challenges.

Of course, online distance learning for students is growing, too. As author Louise Yarnall notes, the reasons students choose "netcourses" are almost as varied as the students themselves. Most are seeking more quality and flexibility in courses than their own schools offer, schools that may not have the resources or student demand to justify adding a particular course. Yarnall looks at programs such as the pioneering Virtual High School, providing a helpful guide to what works and what doesn't in online distance learning, based on her extensive research in the field.

For now, big advances in online distance learning and other web-based resources may have to wait until more schools get access to the Internet2. This alternative, super-high-speed network was set up to bypass the original Internet, which by 2003 was serving an estimated 600 million users worldwide, according to the *New York Times* (Selingo, 2003). In contrast, the Internet2 had just three million users, mostly university researchers, and the ability to move data 1,500 times or more faster than its predecessor. This opens up terrific possibilities for education. Especially promising, the Internet2 will allow high-speed videoconferencing without all the buggy delays, which will change distance learning both for students and teachers.

Yet while 99 percent of elementary and secondary schools had Internet access in 2003, many via sluggish dial-up connections, less than 10 percent (about 7,100) had Internet2 connections. Clearly, the next great effort to close the digital divide will have to focus not on the quantity of Internet connections but on their quality. But even with less-than-ideal technology, one thing is clear: the Digital Classroom is here to stay. For teachers, school administrators, students, and parents, the challenge now is to find ways to make the most of what these marvelous new technological tools have to offer. This book is a good place to start.

Reference

Selingo, J. (2003, August 14). As belated converts, schools keep vigil for Internet2. *New York Times*. Available online at http://partners.nytimes.com/pages/technology/

Multiple Literacies: New Skills for a New Millennium

By Andrea Oseas and Julie M. Wood

It's not unusual to see educators knit their brows at even the most casual mention of "multiple literacies." As a term *du jour,* it is shrouded in ambiguity because of the many concepts it might encompass: media literacy, visual literacy, information literacy, music literacy, multicultural literacy, environmental literacy, and so on. And on a deeper level, teachers are often uncertain about the vast societal transformation looming ahead. What new mountains will they and their students need to scale—and what intellectual skills will that require?

In practical terms, the most compelling questions represent two sides of the same coin: How will teachers, who know how to teach but are not fluent in new technologies, teach students who are fluent with new technologies but don't know how to use them critically?

To answer these questions we first need to clarify what we mean by multiple literacies. Taken broadly, multiple literacies can be conceived as students' ability to identify and analyze messages embedded in a variety of different modalities, as well as the capacity to use these media to create and express their own messages (Aspen Institute, 1997). In today's digital classroom, media literacy, visual literacy, and information literacy are of greatest consequence. Although they overlap considerably, each has unique properties of dissemination and expression.

Media literacy is the flagship of these second-generation literacies, having been around long enough to build a substantial constituency. Initially centered on television, the term *media* has since expanded to include all mass media. Today's media have become so powerful and ubiquitous that cynics have begun referring to them as "weapons of mass persuasion." Given most students' infatuation with their media, especially the entertainment variety, asking them to scrutinize that which brings them intense pleasure is a challenging (and crucial) enterprise.

Although images abound in most mass media, visual literacy has grown into its own field of inquiry. With its language of images and symbols, it is often seen as the companion of textual literacy, especially as the two are often inextricably blended in today's dominant technology, the Internet. In cyberspace, as elsewhere, visual data are encoded with implicit and explicit messages; learning to recognize and interpret them is at the core of the visual literacy curriculum. Equally important, students need to know how to create and manipulate these complex images.

Understanding the language of visual representation may seem counter-literate to some. After all, we are a culture that has historically assessed intelligence using verbal and mathematical measures. But culture took a sharp turn with the wholesale adoption of the Internet coupled with more expansive notions of aptitude, such as Howard Gardner's theory of Multiple Intelligences, which holds that we are all endowed with at least eight distinctive "intelligences," including kinesthetic, musical, and interpersonal (Gardner, 1991). Herein lies a paradox. While visual literacy has risen in stature as a valid and imperative means of understanding the world, we often assume that children will develop these sophisticated skills independently, without explicit instruction on our part. However, it's unrealistic to assume that students will learn to "read" and produce images without some guidance, and it's unreasonable to expect them to succeed in today's media-saturated culture without this ability (Semali, 2002).

Information literacy is perhaps the most unwieldy of the new literacies. As the Internet serves up a smorgasbord of reliable and unreliable information, the need for information literacy has a new urgency. Freed from traditional and institutional gatekeepers, information of varying degrees of integrity travels from one computer to millions of others. Students must learn to locate information that is accurate and appropriate and then use it competently. Once they locate it, they must divine their own path as they are enticed to follow a series of promising links. They must also be able to recognize information that is tainted or fabricated, and understand how it is used to sell, manipulate, and/or exploit.

Rather than approach these three literacies as separate entities, we advocate a more general approach that focuses less on the modalities themselves and more on the overarching skills that are essential to all literacies, traditional and emergent alike.

Why Is It Important?

Though it may seem unfair to ask teachers already straining under the weight of curriculum and standards preparation to master multiple literacies as well, it is becoming increasingly necessary. More than ever before, mass media exert a strong influence on how students see themselves in the broader world (Kellner, 2000). Their opinions, hopes, and dreams are shaped by the stories and images that populate their magazines, televisions, computer screens, and movies. And although the entertainment media transmute violence into entertainment and physical beauty into worthiness, very few incentives encourage students to "look under the hood" for implicit values and messages.

Of course, this is not a new problem. In a capitalist economy, everyone, from little kids to the elderly, is enlisted to keep the market running with a steady diet of consumption. But now, the Internet offers new means of reaching the hearts, minds, and pocketbooks of students. And it is not only commodities for sale: lifestyles, political views, and ideologies are also competing for "customers." The world in which we are preparing our students to live and thrive is one where information arrives at warp speed from electronic media. It is virtually impossible to participate as an informed citizen unless we know how to extract and process information from multiple sources.

To complicate matters, the digital classroom presents a different dynamic than the one for which most teachers have been trained. A growing percentage of students come to class with extensive experience using multiple technologies for social, educational, and recreational purposes, which, in essence, makes them technology experts. The potential for synergy exists if teachers are comfortable letting students mentor them in the latest technologies while they function as learning experts.

As educators, it often feels as though we have lost control over the amount and quality of this information. Given that students are exposed to an ever-expanding range of information purveyors, the key is to shift the focus from becoming more informed to becoming *better* informed. A suitable line of defense against the information surfeit would be to explore ways to leverage new media to accelerate the development of critical skills, in effect converting the problem space into a laboratory (Hobbs, 1998).

On the positive side, new technologies—from instant messaging to "'zines"—give students the opportunity to interact with this newly available information and use it in the construction of their own ideas and expressions. If our ongoing educational objective is to empower students to critique and create, to be comfortable considering and parsing multiple perspectives, we have never before had so many useful tools at our disposal. The important challenge, of course, is learning how to use them well.

Child-Centered Learning

Although it may seem counterintuitive to turn to the past to better understand how to teach in the digital age, in fact the visionary thinkers of long ago can illuminate the present. Consider the educational philosopher John Dewey (1859–1952), for example. One hallmark of progressive education was *child-centered* learning—a radical notion in 1899, when Dewey described these methods. Dewey and other like-minded reformers were determined to free students from the shackles of *subject-centered* schools. They claimed that in such schools a rigid, institutional, authoritarian pedagogy left little room for active learning (Ravitch, 1983).

What Dewey and other supporters of child-centered learning were after was a way for children's own cognitive, social, and emotional needs and interests to drive their teaching and learning. As Linda Darling-Hammond of the Stanford University School of Education remarks, the right software can help teachers use computers to support child-centered inquiry. For example, software such as SimCity can be viewed as "a 21st-century analog of Dewey's 'Let's grow a garden together'" (quoted in Cwiklik, 1997, p. R19).

Others have shared this sentiment. A panel of former President Clinton's top private-sector advisers on education suggested that a progressive (or discovery learning) paradigm offers the most promising model for using computers in today's classrooms (Cwiklik, 1997). The panel offered several ways to foster multiple literacies, such as electronic environments that facilitate group collaboration and interactive encyclopedias that offer multimedia illustrations and relevant links.

In revisiting Dewey's progressive philosophy today, it's clear that new technologies have tremendous potential to support progressive teaching methods. And here's another great advantage—new tools can save teachers untold hours of rushing about gathering resources. A few clicks will often supply more resources than anyone can handle, whether they're dissecting a virtual frog or vicariously exploring the ruins in ancient Rome.

The protean capabilities of new electronic tools for learning breathe new life into Dewey's ideas about discovery learning, and his theories also can help guide their use. Indeed, it is this concretion of established principles and new possibilities that produces some of the most valuable insights about how to proceed.

From Information to Knowledge

Another seminal thinker and philosopher, Swiss genetic epistemologist Jean Piaget (1896–1980), revolutionized the field by launching the "constructivist" or "discovery" learning movement in the 1960s. Piaget's model of learning centered on a child's interactions with the environment (i.e., reading, listening, and exploring). He maintained that young children can be smart, energetic agents of their own conceptual development (Gelman & Brown, 1986), a process that continues over a lifetime. This theory has practical applications for students confronting an onslaught of information outside of the classroom, where they conduct their own research and synthesis.

There is also much to be gleaned by using the constructivist framework in the digital classroom. Brooks and Brooks (1993) suggest four hallmarks of constructivist classrooms that are aligned with the objective of multiple literacies. Constructivist classrooms:

- free students from the tedium of fact-driven curricula and allow them to focus on large ideas
- place in students' hands the exhilarating power to follow trails of interest to make connections, reformulate ideas, and reach unique conclusions
- offer students the important message that the world is a complex place in which multiple perspectives exist and where truth is often a matter of interpretation
- acknowledge that learning and the process of assessing learning are, at best, elusive and messy endeavors that are not easily managed

No pedagogy is better suited than contructivism to the requirements of the information age. By allowing children the freedom to lead their own inquiries, the constructivist model helps children actively participate in the conversion of information into knowledge (Bruce, 2002). In this context, teachers *guide* the learning, and many who are teaching under the intense pressure of performance-based accountability have discovered creative ways to meld the curriculum for standardized tests with the acquisition of learning skills. In the next section we'll discuss how learning can be broken down into the components of *what* and *how*. When teachers have little control over the content, many choose to emphasize how to teach subjects in innovative ways that compound the learning. Yes, many children will be subjected to high-stakes testing.

And yet, when all the tests are over, what matters most is that the child knows how to think and to learn. This is the true measure of an education, and if it fails to nurture these skills, then it has failed our children in the most fundamental way.

Multiple Literacies in Action

In these days of standardized tests, there are teachers who use a constructivist approach to teaching multiple literacies in ways that do in fact develop the competencies everyone is aiming for (i.e., reading, writing, comprehension, content-area studies, etc.).

As an example of a teacher who bridges theory and practice without abandoning the methods that have served her well throughout her career, consider media specialist Valerie Becker, who teaches in an elementary school on Martha's Vineyard, an island off the coast of Massachusetts. A well-respected innovator among her peers, she collaborates with other teachers on ways to use media to teach, inform, and in general enhance all curricular areas. One of Valerie's great strengths is the way she draws upon teachers' expertise in creating media-based projects.

For true inspiration, go to the West Tisbury home page that Valerie helped create and click on "Lauren's Fourth Biographies" (www.wtisbury.mv.k12.ma.us/projects/bioweb/bioindex.htm). You'll see, for example, a student named Beau dressed up as Neil Armstrong. Beau has written a poem that begins, "Neil Armstrong was the first man on the moon/Who feels good to be the first man on the moon." He includes a biography of Armstrong, as well as a timeline and an audio clip of the Beatles' "Penny Lane"—music from Armstrong's era. At first the biographies are merely clever, but as one scrolls down the page, the lives of famous people like Rachel Carson and Jacques Cousteau unfold in impressive detail. Students express their ideas in multiple genres. Ultimately, each biography speaks volumes about the personality of the young biographer and his or her understanding of the world.

For "Martha's Third Grade Pond Project" (www.wtisbury.mv. k12.ma.us/projects/ms_ponds/index.html), Valerie and third-grade teacher Martha Stackpole taught students how to incorporate video, photographs, and informational text about spring peepers into a multimedia study of the local pond. You'll notice that children also contributed original paintings (as in the one that illustrates precipitation, condensation, and evaporation), poems illustrated with digital photos, and animations that accompany "point of view" stories. Again, students create hyperlinks among mixed text genres, with multimedia, to express what they have learned.

Beyond creating presentations and sharing them in ways that transcend classroom walls, students need to know how to negotiate a sophisticated site designed by experts. Take the website "The Rainforest: People, Animals, and Facts" (www.christiananswers.net/kids/rainforest/home.html). An adventurous teacher who dispatches a group of students to conduct research about rainforest animals would soon discover whether they know how to download audio formats, manage the buttons on a digital video player, and "read" a photograph (Coiro, 2003). To be successful, students would need to be fluent in all these facets of literacy. As Don Tapscott has remarked, "Never before has it been more necessary that children learn to read, write, and think critically. It's not just point and click. It's point, read, think, click" (1998; cited in Coiro, 2002, p. 63).

While most students are aficionados of interactive technology, it's important not to lose sight of the impact that older technologies, like television, have on them as well. According to a 1999 Kaiser Family Foundation national study of the media use of over 3,000 children and adolescents, students ages eight and older spend, on average, six and three-quarters hours a day engaged with media outside of school (i.e., watching TV, videos, or movies, listening to CDs, using computers, reading, playing video games). Among children in this age group, two-thirds have a TV in their bedroom; almost half report watching TV during meals. It's safe to assume that most of them are not analyzing this medium that they turn to for entertainment, nor are they trying to decipher television's subtle messages.

To help older students think critically about what they watch, you might have them select a popular program, such as *Law and Order*. Encourage them to watch several episodes, keeping careful track of the types of violence that are portrayed and the number of violent incidents per episode. Students can simultaneously report any stereotypes they detect in the program for further analysis with peers.

Alternatively, you might ask students to conduct a content analysis of the advertisements aired during a particular news program over the course of several days. What are the broadcasters selling? What can we infer about who advertisers envision as their target audience? What techniques do advertisers use to pitch their product? After students analyze their data, you might invite them to create a class presentation to synthesize their main findings.

Learning the Language of Images

"What is the use of a book," thought Alice in Wonderland, "without pictures or conversation?" Indeed. If, as we assert, visual literacy is the companion of textual literacy, then Alice's complaint is not altogether unreasonable. Today's multimedia texts often make lavish use of illustrations, photographs, diagrams, music, and animation. Children are accustomed to books that draw them into other worlds, rendering the

Victorian-era books Alice would have read dull and lifeless by comparison.

How do multimedia texts contribute to or detract from students' ability to construct meaning from a variety of sources? As we teach students to become literate, how can we extend our grasp beyond the written and spoken word?

Imagine classrooms in which visual literacy is woven into the fabric of reading and writing. What do such classrooms look like? One example involves classic art and literature. A teacher might juxtapose artworks that depict Greek and Roman myths and have students "read them" visually as they engage with the myths. Joseph M. Piro (2002) writes eloquently on this subject, describing what happened when he asked fifth graders to analyze paintings such as Pieter Bruegel's *Landscape with the Fall of Icarus* or Rembrandt's *Minerva* as a prelude to reading the corresponding myth. Piro observed that students were able to "enter the work of art," noting the interrelatedness of size, color, and characters. They tried out newly understood words such as texture, hue, and contrast. Ultimately students were asked to write about the myth using this prompt: "You have been asked to write the next chapter in the story of Daedalus and Icarus. Unfreeze the action in the painting and tell what happens" (p. 133).

As Piro reminds us, "Because of early responses to picture books as a first reading experience, children do not think only in written language but in visual images as well" (2000, p. 128). Drawing upon Bloom, Piro adds, "This helps them [students] cross over and discover meaning in nonverbal representations" (p. 128).

In other classrooms, students connect literacy and culture by becoming curators of their own digital art exhibit. While this might sound too complex, the Internet makes ambitious projects like this feasible. Several major museums, such as New York's Metropolitan Museum of

Art (www.metmuseum.org/collections/index.asp), offer a streamlined way for students to select as many as 50 favorite works from their websites and add them to their own "virtual galleries" by gathering them electronically. Students can copy and paste into special gallery spaces or import them directly into a word-processing document.

To take advantage of this opportunity to create cohesive galleries, students will need to use both critical and creative thinking skills. They will need to decide which pieces to group together for their galleries. In addition, they will need to construct a narrative for why they chose the works they did, and how they interpreted and arranged each one to fulfill a personal vision (Wood, 2001). One way to increase the dividends is to give students the opportunity to create their own work for inclusion.

Another way to help students understand and interpret visual images is to have them assemble virtual galleries to address a theme such as "What is beauty?" How will students decide what to include? Whose standards of beauty will they use? What prejudices or cultural stereotypes might be reflected in students' choices? Students' conceptions of beauty may be quite diverse, lending themselves to spirited discussions. One might point out that early conceptions of beauty contrast sharply with those of later eras: For example, compare the hefty stomach and thighs of the *Venus of Willendorf* (witcombe.sbc.edu/willendorf/willendorfdiscovery.html), which was carved between 24,000 and 22,000 BCE in what is now Austria, with the flat-bellied *Venus de Milo* (www.artchive.com/artchive/G/greek/venus_de_milo. jpg.html), which was sculpted in Greece around 130–120 BCE.

How do adolescents define beauty? How can they locate their aesthetic sensibilities? These questions and others that will surely arise will help students examine their own aesthetic and become cultural critics as well as curators of art. Ultimately, we are trying to prepare students to become curators of information in all its forms; to help them become proficient at arranging, organizing, and synthesizing the vast amount of stimuli that animate their lives; and to add their own original ideas to the mix.

From Information to Understanding

In the end, we want students to have learned how to learn. To do so, they need to know "how information is organized, how to find information and how to use information in such a way that others can learn from them" (American Library Association, 1990, p. 1).

Learning how to learn requires that students are able to process and analyze what they read. Thus, comprehension is a cornerstone to information literacy. But consider this fact: Explicit instruction in comprehension skills—not merely questioning students about what they have read, but really demonstrating how to self-monitor what they are learning as they read—is a rare occurrence in many middle-grade classrooms (Pressley, 1998).

We want our students to be able to make meaning on a surface level—for example, to know the country where *Hamlet* is set—and we also want them to develop a deep, analytical understanding of the texts they read. But this proposition raises many conundrums. Modern society is awash in information; a person could be forgiven for disappearing for days while searching on the Internet for a few good, reliable, and informative resources about, say, the solar system. How can we help students become effective researchers, researchers who are engaged with the topics they're studying, researchers who bring a genuine curiosity to their quest for information?

Inquiry learning offers teachers one of the most promising strategies for motivating students to conduct research. This approach is ideal for having students work individually or collaboratively to find answers to questions they themselves have devised related to curricular themes —from the history of the Parthenon to the life cycle of a sea urchin. Not only is this teaching method one that has gained currency among teachers over the years, it is also particularly well suited to using technological tools. In researching their questions, students can use multimedia encyclopedias and other CD-ROMs, as well as carefully targeted websites. Similarly, students can use presentation tools that incorporate hypertext, graphic software, and timelines to help them assimilate and communicate their ideas. Thus, if one's own questions offer a *raison d'être* for reading, writing, and understanding, technology contributes tools that are the other half of the equation.

As Marcus Aurelius (121–180 CE) observed, "There is nothing Nature loves so well as to change existing forms and to make new ones like them." No sooner have we mastered one technology than another comes along. But it's not just the technological landscape that is evolving; our assumptions of what it means to be educated are also in flux. While we adjust to rapid change, we need to keep our eyes on the ball— helping students engage fully and creatively with their world. We must also help them find their compass in the cascade of messages and competing values ushered in by the information age.

Fortunately we already have expertise in developing the core abilities that are essential for all literacies—they just need to be flexed and stretched in new directions. Progressive teaching methods that have served us well in the past are as applicable today as ever; we need only re-envision what we already know about learning. If we can approach multiple literacies with critical and creative elasticity, we open up new possibilities for invigorated explorations of what is and what can be.

References

American Library Association Presidential Committee on Information Literacy. (1990). *Final reports*. Chicago: American Library Association.

Aspen Institute. (1997). Media literacy: A report of the National Leadership Conference on Media Literacy. In R. Kubey (Ed.), *Media literacy in the information age* (vol. 6, pp. 79–86). New Brunswick, NJ: Transaction.

Brooks, J. G., & Brooks, M. G. (1993). *In search of understanding: The case of constructivist classrooms*. Alexandria, VA: Association for Supervision and Curriculum Development.

Bruce, B. C. (2002). Diversity and social engagement: How changing technologies enable new modes of literacy in changing circumstances. In D. E. Alvermann (Ed.), *Adolescents and literacies in a digital world* (pp. 1–18). New York: Peter Lang.

Coiro, J. (2003). Exploring literacy on the Internet. *Reading Teacher, 56,* 458–464.

Cwiklik, R. (1997, November 17). Dewey wins! *Wall Street Journal,* p. R19.

Durkin, D. (1978–1979). What classroom observations reveal about reading comprehension instruction. *Reading Research Quarterly, 15,* 481–533.

Gardner, H. (1991). *The unschooled mind.* New York: HarperCollins.

Gelman, R., & Brown, A. L. (1986). Changing views of cognitive competence in the young. In N. J. Smelser & D. R. Gerstein (Eds.), *Behavioral and social science: 50 years of discovery* (pp. 175–207). Washington, DC: National Academies Press.

Hobbs, R. (1998). The seven great debates in the media literacy movement. *Journal of Communication, 48*(1), 16–32.

Kaiser Family Foundation. (1999, November 17). *New study finds kids spend equivalent of full work week using media.* Retrieved July 1, 2003 from http://www.kff.org/content/1999/1535/pressreleasefinal.doc.html

Kellner, D. (2000). Multiple literacies and critical pedagogies. In P. P. Trifonas (Ed.), *Revolutionary pedagogy: Cultural politics, instituting education, and the discourse of theory* (pp. 196–221). New York: Routledge.

Piro, J. M. (2002, October) The picture of reading: Deriving meaning in literacy through image. *Reading Teacher, 56*, 126–134.

President's Committee of Advisors on Science and Technology: Panel on Educational Technology. (1997). *Report to the president on the use of technology to strengthen K–12 education in the United States.* Washington, DC: Author.

Pressley, M. (1998). *Reading instruction that works.* New York: Guilford Press.

Ravitch, D. (1983). *The troubled crusade.* New York: Basic Books.

Semali L. (2002). Defining new literacies in curricular practice. *Reading Online, 5*(4). Available online at http://www.readingonline.org

Tapscott, D. (1998). *Growing up digital: The rise of the net generation.* New York: McGraw-Hill.

Wood, J. M. (2001, January/February). Virtual art, real learning. *Instructor,* p. 80.

Ways Technology Can Improve Assessment and Accountability

By David Niguidula

Joe Maruszczak had a dilemma. As principal at Ponaganset High School in Rhode Island, he had just spent a year with his faculty developing the school's "Expectations for Student Learning." Through a great deal of hard work and consensus building, the faculty created—and agreed to—a set of Learning Outcomes that each student would need to demonstrate prior to graduation. But now that the list was approved, a difficult decision lay ahead: *How* could each student demonstrate that he or she met the expectations?

Meanwhile, across the state, Principal Elizabeth Durfee at Primrose Hill Elementary School was thinking about parent-teacher conferences. Twice a year, teachers met with parents to review each child's progress. Together, the teachers and parents reviewed samples of student work. However, it was often difficult for teachers to convey certain aspects of a child's development—particularly in reading and social interaction. Mrs. Durfee wondered, "How can we better communicate a student's progress to the parents?"

In Harrisburg, Pennsylvania, Deputy Superintendent Julie Botel was also thinking about literacy. As in other urban districts, a large percentage of the students were not performing well on state assessments of reading and writing. Of course, there were many reasons for this, and the district brought in a number of programs and initiatives to improve student achievement. To assist the teachers with issues of literacy and to provide ongoing professional development, the district hired reading specialists and instructional facilitators to work with teachers on site in each school. But how could the facilitators help teachers diagnose their students' needs?

Each of these stories is about an issue of assessment and accountability. Educators across the globe are wrestling with similar questions as they think about issues of teaching and learning while attempting to meet the demands of state accountability systems.

Technology, of course, can be of help: Computers were designed to help people store, retrieve, communicate, and organize large amounts of information. Each of the schools mentioned above used digital portfolios as a way of addressing this concern. However, solving the dilemmas of assessment requires more than finding the right program. Educators need to think about how the information will be collected and reported—and how teachers, students, parents, and administrators can analyze and reflect on that information.

In this chapter, we will examine how schools can think about using technology for assessment and accountability. There is a set of key questions that schools should address:

- What is our purpose?
- What information do we really need?
- How do we collect the information?
- How do we communicate the information?

- How do we reflect on the information?

Let's take each of these in turn.

What Is Our Purpose?

Before a school implements any technology initiative, its faculty and administration need to decide on its educational purpose. For example, when Joe Maruszczak and the faculty at Ponaganset High School thought about how students could demonstrate the school's Learner Expectations, they knew that any system would have to support two purposes. First, the system should encourage teachers to connect individual assignments (and their course as a whole) to particular expectations. Second, the system should encourage students to express their individuality. The system needed to be more than a checklist where students crossed Expectations off a list; rather, it needed to help students tell their own stories about how they achieved these outcomes. In general, the system needed to turn the Expectations from a list on a piece of paper into a part of the school culture.

The result is a web-based digital portfolio. Figure 1 shows the main menu for the portfolio. On the left are the nine Learner Expectations; the reader can click on any of these buttons and see the list of how the student has demonstrated that particular expectation. In the main table of the screen, we see that one of the Expectations ("demonstrate an ability to listen, read, and process information effectively") consists of two Learning Outcomes. Students can create entries for the portfolio at each grade level; to do so, they make a link from this menu page to their student work. (Students are also asked to annotate their work, indicating why they believe that a particular entry should be linked to these Expectations.)

Figure I   Main Menu for Ponaganset High School Digital Portfolio

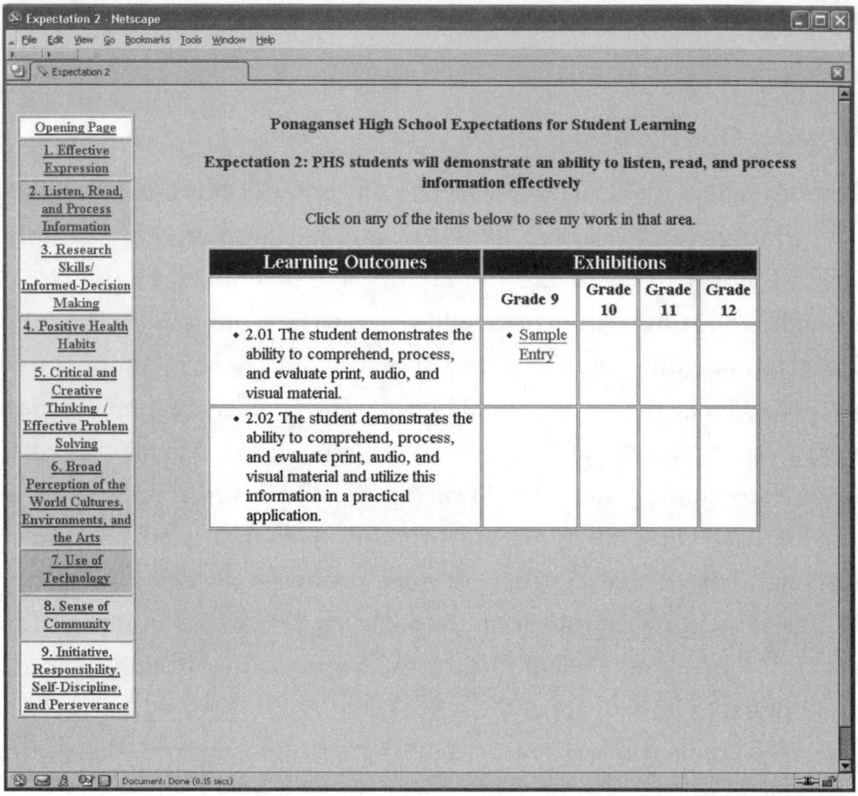

The design of this screen reflects the school's purposes. By using the Learner Expectations as the organizing structure, students and teachers are compelled to think about how any given piece of work is connected to the Expectations. The design also allows the reader to see, at a glance, if there are any gaps in the Expectations that the student has met.

Of course, there are a variety of technological tools that can be useful for assessment. Most student information systems now have modules to help collect the data to meet state and federal policy regulations. When reviewing such systems, educators should consider if the same information can be easily reported to teachers and principals. After all, teachers should be able to use such information for their own improvement.

In the classroom, there are tools that help with observing students. For example, Sunburst's *Learner Profile* and Wireless Generation's *mClass* both run on personal digital assistants (PDAs). Using these tools, teachers can record observational data about students to supplement other academic work. *Learner Profile* can be used to indicate when students are playing well with others, and *mClass* helps teachers collect information such as running records.

There are, of course, tools to support traditional assessments. Indeed, the technology used to scan pencil marks on a bubble sheet has been around since the 1940s, and is one of the most enduring elements of educational technology. A number of products (including several websites) help teachers create, score, and record multiple-choice or other types of basic assessments.

What Information Do We Really Need?

Technology allows us to capture information that wasn't easily available before. With scanners, digital cameras, and sound recording equipment, just about anything that students create can be stored in digital form. Gigabytes of data can be made available on every desktop in a district. But just because it is possible to capture more and different kinds of data doesn't mean that schools should try to capture everything. Being selective about the data to collect will help schools save the resource often in shortest supply: time.

At Primrose Hill School, the faculty began their work with digital portfolios by thinking about their parent-teacher conferences. The faculty knew that they wanted to demonstrate student literacy skills over time, and thus decided to record samples of reading and writing in the portfolio. A sample of a first grader's portfolio appears in Figure 2.

Figure 2 shows a reading sample. Twice a year, before the fall and spring teacher conferences, the students are asked to read for the teacher. In the portfolio, the screen shows three things about the reading: the text read by the child, a video clip showing the child reading (and answering comprehension questions about the text), and the teacher's comments about the student's reading. Similarly, a writing sample contains the prompt given by the teacher, a scanned version of the student's work, and the teacher's reflections.

Initially the Primrose faculty wanted to capture the student reading an entire text, which would typically take five to eight minutes. But, after recording—and playing back—a few of these video segments, the teachers realized that a much shorter sample (about 60 seconds) told them as much about the reading as the longer piece. Similarly, rather than scanning all of the student writing that was being collected in the paper portfolio, the faculty decided to focus on two representative pieces—the fall and spring quarter writing prompts. These two writing samples allow parents to see growth over time, but minimize the amount of time needed to create the digital portfolio.

The question of "What information do we really need?" is not limited to portfolios. School databases are bursting with information about student test scores, attendance, schedules, grades, free-or-reduced-lunch status, and health records. Of course, schools need to collect a great deal of information to comply with various state and federal regulations. But when it comes to doing their own analyses of student performances, many districts make the mistake of trying to collect too much data—extensive survey forms that are both redundant and time-wasting.

Figure 2   Reading Sample

A number of research projects have created structures to help with collecting and analyzing data. Victoria Bernhardt's School Portfolio provides a framework for helping schools collect data around continuous improvement. The Annenberg Institute for School Reform has posted a set of protocols on line to help schools conduct effective surveys and closely examine student work. The Quality School Portfolio from UCLA's National Center for Research on Evaluation, Standards, and Student Testing (CRESST) is available for schools to collect and analyze data from a variety of sources.

In the end, what ultimately matters is that a school gathers the data that will provide confidence in the conclusions it wants to reach. Data gathering can become an end in itself; schools need to continually revisit their purpose and ask if each point of data is truly useful.

How Do We Collect the Information?

Only after a school has established its purpose and determined what information it wants to collect should the school determine what technology it wants to use. Technology should be driven by the educational needs—not the other way around.

The digital portfolios we have seen in this chapter are web-based templates. Students are given a "shell" of a portfolio, containing the standards they need to meet and the prompts they must respond to. The students' job is first to digitize their work and then to link the work into the portfolio. Students have learned how to link their work into a portfolio very easily; once the work is digitized, the students can link it into the portfolio with just a few keystrokes. (Newer versions of the portfolio, which use web-based forms, are even easier and require less time to add an entry.)

What does take time, however, is the digitizing of the work in the first place. Whether students need to scan a document, type a paper into a word processor, or insert a multimedia clip, a block of time has to be allocated for students to put their work into the computer. Schools have had the most success when the information is created digitally in the first place. If students routinely word process their papers, then adding the work to a digital portfolio is simply a matter of inserting a file. At Primrose Hill, when it came time to capture video of student reading samples, the teachers decided to film an individual assessment that they were going to be doing anyway.

To the degree possible, the process of data collection should fit within a teacher's normal routine. The best strategy is to determine which assessments are most likely to be included in the portfolio—and then provide enough access to technology so that the student work can be recorded digitally as it is being created. The goal is to use the technology as an opportunity to enhance what the teachers would regularly be doing, rather than asking them to spend more time doing data entry.

How Do We Communicate the Information?

Portfolios need to have an audience. In our experience, schools that create a specific time or process for reviewing portfolios get a better response rate than those that simply assume that building a portfolio is enough. The audience does not have to be large; students might know that their work is being presented to a single teacher, or to a parent, or to a peer. But if students know that their work is going to be shown to a particular individual, they tend to be more conscious of the portfolio's appearance and completeness.

Thus, schools need to establish a specific mechanism for showing portfolios or other assessment data. Parent-teacher conferences (or student-led conferences) is one way to show portfolios. Other schools have used open houses, in which students walk through the contents of their portfolios with parents or teachers who are invited to the session. At Barrington High School in Rhode Island, digital portfolios were used as part of the senior project; the portfolio describing each student's field-work and research paper was made available electronically to the judges on that senior's panel.

The critical factor, however, in presenting the information in a portfolio is to work in *layers*. At University Heights High School in the Bronx, which was one of the pilot schools in the original 1994–1997 digital portfolio project, students wrote cover letters describing how each piece of work was connected to one of the school's "domains of knowledge." From this cover letter, readers could go on to review the individual elements of the student's work in more depth. In the Barrington senior project, each segment of the digital portfolio began with a journal entry describing that segment of the project. From that point, the reader could review all of the information from that segment, or move on to the next segment.

Similarly, other forms of assessment data must be presented in a way that will not simply overwhelm the audience. Complex charts and graphs can be very effective in conveying a great deal of information, but an electronic slide presentation of one chart after another leads to information overload. Often, it is more helpful to break a graphic into pieces and present it one segment at a time.

The assessment and accountability information should be used to present a story. In the case of web-based portfolios, students are well aware that this medium can be used to express their individuality; they look for a way to change the colors and fonts of the presentation to show their own personalities. As with many other forms of authentic assessment, knowing that a reader will be taking this work seriously motivates students to take their own work seriously.

How Do We Reflect on the Information?

The assessment data that schools collect should not only tell us about where student performance has been, but also provide clues as to where we want performance to go. For the data to be useful as a diagnostic tool, however, educators have to be able to share the data—and learn how to reflect on the data.

Students using digital portfolios have the opportunity to reflect on their own work. After selecting their work, students are asked, "Why did you put this piece in the portfolio?" or "How do you think this work met the standards?" Often, students initially respond by saying, "I did well because I got a good grade." The key to reflection, however, is to go deeper. Why did this piece get a good grade? What was it about this piece of work that was better than others the student has done in the past? What are the qualities of this work that make it "good"? The teachers who prompt students to reflect on their work are helping students to understand how standards are translated into practice.

A similar process of reflection can help teachers improve their practice. In Harrisburg, the digital portfolios being used in grades K–8 focus on literacy. In some schools, samples of student reading are recorded with a digital camera, and the recording, the text, and a running record are added to a portfolio. (In other schools, the focus is on writing or oral presentations.) Once the sample was added to the portfolio, it was reviewed twice. Both the classroom teacher and the school's reading specialist reviewed the student samples, and both added comments to the portfolio. Sometimes the teacher and reading specialist worked together; sometimes, the comments were added separately. Either way, the teacher—and the student—received the benefit of a second opinion. The district's reading specialists and instructional facilitators are engaged in introducing new ideas about the teaching of reading and writing to the district. The digital portfolio has become an opportunity to reflect on how teachers are reaching each child. It also gives the reading specialists an opportunity to provide individualized professional development to faculty members.

Of course, schools spend a lot of time these days poring over other types of assessment data. Reflecting on numeric data can be tricky; for example, educators might make a conclusion based on disaggregated samples in which groups are too small to be statistically significant. Schools may find it more valuable to use the data as a way of testing hypotheses put forth by teachers as well as administrators. By helping to formulate the questions, teachers may become more engaged with responding to the answers.

In the end, the act of reflecting on the data may be the most crucial part of the process. Technology can be extraordinarily helpful in capturing the work of schools in new ways and providing new views of student achievement. Still, the ultimate key to school improvement comes not from the accumulated stores of data about the students, but through the continuous effort of the school's adults to learn what is best for each student.

For Further Information

Annenberg Institute for School Reform. (2001). *Toolbox for accountability.* Providence, RI: Author. Available online at http://www.annenberg institute.org/Toolbox

Bernhardt, V. L. (1999). *The school portfolio: A comprehensive framework for school improvement* (2nd ed.). Larchmont, NY: Eye on Education.

Ideas Consulting [Website]. (2003). *Sample digital portfolios.* Available online at http://www.ideasconsulting.com/dp

Learner Profile [Computer software]. (2002). Boston: Houghton Mifflin. Available online at www.learnerprofile.com

mClass [Computer software]. (2002). New York: Wireless Generation. Available online at http://www.wgen.net

Niguidula, D., & Davis, H. (2003, March). Giving students the data. *Classroom Leadership, 6*(6), 7.

Niguidula, D. (1997, November). Picturing performance with digital portfolios. *Educational Leadership, 55*(3), 26–29.

Quality school portfolio [Computer software]. (2002). Los Angeles: National Center for Research on Evaluation, Standards, and Student Testing (CRESST). Available online at http://qsp.cse.ucla.edu

Salpeter, J. (2002, January). Accountability: Meeting the challenge with technology. *Technology and Learning, 22*(6), 20–33.

Wolf, D. P. (2002, December). When raising isn't rising. *School Administrator, 59*(11), 20–23.

Plagiarism.k12.us: What Educators Can Do About It

By Michael Sadowski

Adultery, betrayal, promiscuity, subterfuge, and intrigue, all of which would make an excellent coming attraction on the Hollywood scene and probably a pretty good book. Add Puritan ideals and writing styles, making it long, drawn out, tedious, wearisome, sleep inducing, insipidly asinine, and the end result is *The Scarlet Letter*. Despite all these things it is considered a classic and was a statement of the era.

This biting commentary on Nathaniel Hawthorne's novel is from a student book review that can be found on no fewer than a dozen websites, with addresses such as instant-essays.com, digitaltermpapers.com, electronicreferences.com, and killer-essays. com. Some sites display the full text of the paper with no payment required. Others, such as Electronic References, provide an excerpt and require paid registration before a student can view the paper in its entirety; still others charge on a per-paper basis. Regardless of the financial costs involved, students who are able to pass these papers off as their own are—at least in part—getting a free ride on their education.

A Proliferation of Online Term Paper Sites

A 2001 survey of 2,294 high school students conducted by Donald McCabe of Rutgers University's Management Education Center found that more than half admitted to having plagiarized from Internet sources, and the proliferation of online "term paper mills" has made this kind of cheating increasingly easy to do. Experts point to literally thousands of websites from which students can either download or cut and paste papers on a wide variety of school subjects. One site, essayresearch.com (which can also be reached via the more bluntly named web address houseofcheat.com) boasts papers in 26 categories ranging from accounting, agriculture, and art to sociology, sciences, and sports. Some sites even include college application essays, along with those on topics frequently covered in high school and middle school curricula. For situations in which prewritten essays don't quite fit the requirements of an assignment, a number of sites also offer custom-written papers for a per-page fee, which usually varies based on delivery time. For example, a desperate student can order a custom essay from directessays.com for $38 per page and receive it in less than 24 hours.

Most of the websites that sell prewritten and custom-written student papers claim that their purpose is not to facilitate cheating but to provide students with research resources that they can then use to create their own original work. On its homepage, for example, directessays. com posts the following stern warning: "The papers contained within our web site are for research purposes only! You may not turn in our papers as your own work! You must cite our website as your source!" The caveat on killer-essays.com is somewhat friendlier, even teacher-like: "We care for you, the student, so please do not copy, steal, or plagiarize our essays because cheating is wrong and teachers know about this website." One site has even integrated an admonition against plagiarism into its name, nocheaters.com. Nevertheless, this site promises "term papers made easy" and offers "20,000 prewritten models of term papers, essays and reports on every academic subject imaginable," as well as custom-written "model" papers for $29.95 per page, which can be charged to a major credit card.

Fighting Technology with Technology

Given this online landscape—rife with temptations for undermotivated, confused, or procrastinating students—educators face a variety of new challenges in the fight against plagiarism. All educators would agree on the need to discourage students from using the Internet as a source of unoriginal work, but doing so effectively requires a combination of approaches, some of which are more controversial than others.

Perhaps the most direct way to fight online plagiarism is to fight technology with technology. Many teachers use search engines such as Google to identify plagiarized work, entering key words or suspicious strings of text from a student's paper into the search engine to see if similar language appears somewhere on the Internet.

Deborah Holman, a history teacher for the past eight years at Newton North High School in Newton, Massschusetts, says that Google searches have helped her trace a few pieces of suspect student work to term paper mills, but also to more "respectable" sources such as Time.com's history pages and university professors' websites. "I catch maybe one or two blatant instances [of plagiarism] every year," she says. These cases are not limited to students who are simply looking for an easy way out, she notes:

It's sometimes honors kids who are under pressure, who want to perform, and who are afraid that what they're going to produce isn't good enough.

Although not as plentiful as the Internet term paper sites, online resources have also sprung up that are specifically designed to help teachers identify work that has been borrowed from other sources. One of the best known of such sites, turnitin.com, is used throughout the California State University system and by every university in the United Kingdom, according to the company that operates it, iParadigms of Oakland, California. An offshoot of plagiarism.org, a more generalized website dedicated to providing "the latest information on online plagiarism," turnitin.com offers educators at all levels targeted help in identifying whether a particular paper is wholly original. For a registration fee, which averages 60 cents per student for a one-year subscription, teachers can submit a paper and receive an "originality report" that either supports the paper's authenticity or highlights sections that appear to have been plagiarized. About half of the service's subscribers work in higher education and half are K–12 educators, according to cofounder and iParadigms CEO John Barrie.

Barrie says that turnitin.com saves teachers time and targets plagiarism more effectively than general search engines like Google: "Maybe Google is effective to ferret out some students who cheated, but by searching Google you only have time to target a few papers," he notes. "And you're probably going to falsely target some who didn't [cheat]." Barrie also says that his company's databases include resources to which a general search engine would not have access, including subscription-based journals, books, and all student papers ever submitted to turnitin.com, which the company retains so that future submissions can be checked against them.

Debating the Ethics of Plagiarism Detection

The plagiarism detection component of turnitin.com works by using algorithms to create a "digital fingerprint" of any paper submitted. But it is just this sort of language that makes some observers uneasy. As Nick Carbone, a writing instructor and director of new media for Bedford/St. Martin's, stated in a 2001 essay:

> Their model [turnitin.com] is to police your students, through surveillance (constant surveillance if you have every draft of every student's paper uploaded to the site). The counterargument to turnitin.com's heavy-handed approach is that smart assignment design, teaching students how to handle sources, and regular discussions (not harangues) in courses about plagiarism, cheating, and why academic honesty matter are better pedagogic alternatives to constant policing.

Carbone and others have also expressed concern that the submission of papers to turnitin.com violates students' rights vis-à-vis the use of their own work, especially when papers are submitted without their knowledge or consent. Moreover, Carbone challenges an approach he says is based primarily on mistrust of students: "Turnitin.com doesn't allow for trust; it says we don't trust you. It says we're checking up on every draft. It's trying to stop plagiarism primarily by making it impossible to do."

Barrie says the company's practice of retaining student papers is well within the bounds of "fair use," and he refutes the contention that turnitin.com represents a "policing" of student work that is unfair or inconsistent with best practices in teaching. Rather, he says, the service ultimately helps teachers duly reward "the majority of students who are honest," especially given the pervasiveness of cheating made evident by the Rutgers study. "You can talk all you want about better teaching and increased teacher vigilance and honor codes, but if the status quo were working, you wouldn't see the level of plagiarism we're seeing now," he contends. "Are we going to tolerate this problem for the next 20 years while we reform education?"

A Sampling of Solutions

Regardless of teachers' opinions about the best way to prevent plagiarism, most would probably agree that education can be a powerful deterrent when approached effectively. First and most important, of course, students need to be taught how to cite sources correctly—to deprive students of such knowledge is practically to invite them to plagiarize. Second, the very technology that enables widespread plagiarism—the Internet—is also a source of innumerable ideas about how to prevent it. Following is a sampling of strategies drawn from a variety of online sources (with attribution, of course) that offer teachers advice for combating cheating:

- In an online essay entitled "Anti-Plagiarism Strategies for Research Papers," Robert Harris, author of *The Plagiarism Handbook*, recommends that teachers begin by understanding the reasons why students plagiarize. Among these reasons, Harris says, are "poor time management and planning skills," "fear that their writing ability is inadequate," the tendency for students to be "natural economizers," and even "the thrill of rule breaking." Addressing all of these issues directly with students—without even talking about their connections to plagiarism—might actually reduce the temptation to borrow from online sources in the first place (see http://www.virtualsalt.com/antiplag.html).

- In a piece written for the online education 'zine *From Now On: The Educational Technology Journal*, editor and former librarian Jamie McKenzie suggests that teachers avoid the kinds of assignments that might encourage students to "binge" on online information. Instead of general information reports (what McKenzie calls "trivial pursuits"), he recommends giving more assignments that require explanation, problem-solving, and decisionmaking and are centered around essential questions (see "The New Plagiarism: Seven Antidotes to Prevent Highway Robbery in an Electronic Age," http://www.fno.org/may98/cov98may.html).

- Working students through the writing process is a strategy recommended in a variety of online sources. If teachers are able to monitor a student's work through such steps as brainstorming, organizing information, outlining, and multiple drafts, it is less likely that he or she could "successfully" plagiarize a final product. Lisa Hinchliffe of the University of Illinois at Urbana–Champaign recommends that teachers require students to submit such things as "topic proposals, idea outlines, multiple drafts, interim working bibliographies and photocopies of sources" (see "Cut-and-Paste Plagiarism: Preventing, Detecting and Tracking Online Plagiarism" at http://alexia.lis.uiuc.edu/~janicke/plagiary.htm). However, some aspects of process writing require educators to be more—not less—vigilant about plagiarism, says the "Addressing Plagiarism" web page published by the Writing Center at the University of Washington, Bothell: "The increasing emphasis on process writing, in the form of peer critiques, visits to the writing center, and multiple drafts of essays, can render the line between plagiarism and collaboration and the boundaries that define intellectual private property unclear at best for both instructors and students" (see http://www.bothell. washington.edu/writingcenter/writing/plagiarism.html).

- Giving students a "dry run" in using information sources and then writing about them can be a way to teach about acceptable use and to monitor where students might unwittingly cross the line into plagiarism. The online article "An Antidote to Plagiarism" by Anthony Cody of the Oakland (Calif.) Unified School District contains such a step-by-step lesson (along with a sample information source) for grades 5–10 (see http:// tlc.ousd.k12. ca.us/~acody/antidote.html).

- Engaging students in challenging, technology-based assignments that directly educate about plagiarism can also lessen the need for teacher admonitions or stern referrals to the student handbook. For example, Lynne Schalman of the Noble and Greenough School in Dedham, Mass. (which enrolls students in grades 7–12), has created a curriculum for a web quest called "Avoiding Plagiarism." In Schalman's lesson, each of three groups researches a different aspect of plagiarism online: the difference between plagiarism and acceptable paraphrasing; the various actions that constitute plagiarism; and prevention and detection. Each group is given a set of web links and is then required to create a PowerPoint presentation based on its findings (see http://www.teachingcompany. com/plagiarismwebquest/ index.htm).

- Elaine Razzano, one of the "cybermentors" on the National Council of Teachers of English (NCTE) anti-plagiarism website, recommends adding a component to all research assignments that requires students to submit written evaluations for any web sources they use. "This added requirement forces students to slow down and to think critically about their sources," Razzano notes (see http://www.ncte.org/solutions/plagiarism_ cyberbrief.shtml).

Central to most of the antiplagiarism tips available on the Internet is the commonsense notion that once students understand what plagiarism is—and is not—they will be less likely to fall victim to its temptations. Cultivating such an understanding, of course, requires time, a commodity that is scarce in many schools—where tests are driving more and more of the content that is taught. Still, as long as online plagiarism continues to be a problem from the elementary grades through graduate school, few tasks seem more important than teaching students to respect the integrity of their own and others' work.

References

Carbone, N. (2001, December 3). *Thinking and talking about plagiarism*. Bedford/St. Martin's Tech Notes. Retrieved September 4, 2003, from http://bedfordstmartins.com/technotes/techtiparchive/ttip102401.htm

McCabe, D. (2001). Cheating: Why students do it and how we can help them stop. *American Educator, 25*(4), 38–43.

Building Better School-Home Connections with Technology

By Kristi Rennebohm Franz

J ust as new technologies are transforming K–12 classroom practice, they also are providing opportunities to strengthen school-home connections. Email, websites, digital photos, video, and other such innovations enable students to demonstrate their work to parents through visual, aural, and written means. This in turn gives parents a better understanding of what takes place in classrooms—of what students and teachers do and learn, the context of that work, and the conversations and collaborations they have with both local and global learning partners—and lay the groundwork for helpful student-parent-teacher discussions.

As parents become better informed about school learning, they can support their children's educational journey in ways not previously possible. With new technologies, we can bring classroom experiences into the homes of students to provide a rich context for parents and their students to talk about school learning.

Both educational research and classroom experience tell us that opportunities for positive and ongoing communication and collaboration between school and home are essential to successful K–12 education. They energize the educational process. Never before have we had such opportunities to generate new traditions of student, parent, and teacher communication and collaboration. In response to the old familiar question from parents—"What did you do in school today?"—students are able to share their school experiences with their parents through technology. They can take their parents to the classroom website to show them the work they did that day in the classroom, or sit down with them to view a class-produced video documentary of important learning experiences. They may share email communications on curricular topics that are being sent and received from global peers with whom the class is doing collaborative online project learning. These documents become a basis for detailed conversations about school learning between parents and their children and, as such, can significantly strengthen school-home relationships.

New Traditions in the Classroom

Creating new traditions of student-parent-teacher collaborations must begin in the classroom. In our primary classroom in eastern Washington (see page 50 for web address), new technologies are seamlessly integrated across the curricula. These technologies are used by all students, across a diversity of learning styles and profiles of progress. Whether in individual, small-group, or whole-class lessons, every student is an active participant and has ownership in project-based classroom learning across all content areas. Students are taught to use new technologies to do projects in science, math, social studies, literacy, world languages, visual arts, and service learning. They also collaborate with peers and teachers worldwide through such programs as the International Education and Resource Network (iEARN), the Peace Corps World Wise

Schools program, and the Global Learning and Observation to Benefit the Environment (GLOBE) project.

Using email, students write to global peers about curricular topics and read their responses. They learn to select and edit digital photos to illustrate their writing. Web publishing software lets them post their work on the classroom website. Video editing software for producing video documentaries of project learning experiences and presentation software enables them to prepare videoconference workshops with collaborating schools in distant locations.

Desktop publishing gives students opportunities to bring their experiences and ideas into print with illustrations easily and efficiently, providing visible and concrete evidence of their success in meeting educational goals. We then use these documents to mentor students in reflecting on their work and revising it for greater accuracy and completeness. This process of generating documents for learning is a safe and inviting one for students. As students look at their work in positive collaboration with peers and the teacher, they are open to suggestions for revision; they willingly talk about what they want to change and what they want to be able to do.

As students experience a continual process of reviewing and revising their work in the classroom, they learn to clearly articulate what works, what doesn't, and what they can do to make changes and improvements in their documents. This collaborative process of reflection and revision helps them confidently explain to their parents (or others at home) the process of creating their classroom project documents.

New Traditions at Home

These new traditions of collaboration extend beyond the school classroom. Students, who are typically eager to share their classroom activities with people at home, write notes informing their parents that new web pages have been posted online. Parents can "visit" the classroom website using home computers or those of a public library. The online documents and classroom videos provide powerful prompts for students to talk with their parents about school experiences. As authors and "owners" of the website documents, they can explain the steps in the lessons, how the schoolwork was accomplished, and what they learned. These conversations give parents a good sense of what their children are trying to accomplish in the classroom. Parents learn about the process and see the finished products of their children's schoolwork.

By viewing documents and videos created at school, parents join the classroom learning community. Teacher-authored pages on the classroom website explain the classroom curricula and education goals so parents can understand learning expectations and teaching practice (Rennebohm Franz, 2000a, 2000b, 2000c, 2000d, 2000e, 2000f, 2000g). Parents have an excellent "view" of their student as an active and productive learner.

New Traditions in At-School Meetings

The result of these school-to-home collaborations is productive communication that is 1) focused on student work and 2) supports and recognizes student achievement. This makes at-school meetings more productive, too. When parents come to school for classroom open house evenings, family computer nights, and student-parent-teacher report card conferences, they have the opportunity see the real classroom context that is documented on the website. Students demonstrate uses of software programs to their parents and show the full array of classroom materials used in curricular learning, including books, math tools, science activities, globes, atlases, musical instruments, and art materials.

As students present their classroom to their parents, parents recognize that what they have seen of the classroom "on the screen" represents many of the traditional activities one would expect to see in a primary classroom. Students are reading books, drawing and creating artwork, using math manipulatives, completing "paper-pencil" writing activities, doing helper chart assignments, and working individually or collaboratively with peers to accomplish tasks. They are also having one-on-one, small-group, and whole-class instruction in learning centers around the room, including a science table, geography center, and library center.

Added to traditional learning experiences is the fact that their children know how to use new technologies to 1) capture their learning experiences in computer documents, 2) work with revising and improving those documents to better understand and present curricular concepts, and 3) communicate those documents to global peers in distant locations to further extend their learning. Parents see that their children's uses of new technologies are purposeful and that using these technologies for school-home collaborations is creating a real sense of community around student learning.

Family computer nights are planned throughout the school year to give parents and students time to use the computer lab and classroom computers together. An important purpose of these events is for students to show their parents the details and tools of how they use productivity software in curricular learning. With greater time and access to computers than is possible at open-house events, students can show parents how they do their work with new technologies, parents can try the tools, and together they can talk about what can be learned using computers. The teacher can circulate around the room to answer parents' questions and provide information on the teaching strategies and goals behind the student work.

An equally important purpose of the family computer night is to demonstrate to parents the purposeful educational uses of new technologies so they will encourage children to use these tools at home or at the public library. For example, as students show their parents how we use desktop tools to complete the writing process (prewrite, draft, edit, revise, and publish), parents learn how to mentor writing at home (Rennebohm Franz, 2000f, 2000g). As parents see that students' email correspondence with global peers is an important component of learning to read and write, they urge their children to compose and send email to friends and family members as a way to build literacy skills at home. With a better understanding of how students work on the classroom website, parents can use these online documents to help students outside of school. Such sessions make both parents and students more inclined to go on line together for educational purposes.

For parents with limited opportunities to visit classrooms, new technologies offer a way to participate more fully in their children's education. Parents are not just recipients of test scores and report cards, but they can also follow their student's learning process through email, websites, video, and videoconference documents. However, in building school-home partnerships, new technologies should supplement, not replace, face-to-face conversations with parents. Real-time opportunities for students, parents, and teachers to talk together in the classroom are still essential and irreplaceable foundations for trusted collaborations.

At our school, report card conferences are an important part of these efforts to establish new traditions of school-home collaboration. During the week prior to conferences, students prepare portfolios of schoolwork, including plans to demonstrate and review computer documents. Students come to the conference with their parents prepared to show their portfolios and talk about their learning progress and plans.

Unlike traditional report card conferences, where parents and students anxiously await the unveiling of grades and progress reports by the teachers, our new tradition of collaboration has parents, teachers, and students eagerly looking forward to conference times.

Why? Because there are few surprises at the conferences. Through their access to classroom websites and class-produced videos, as well as open-house events and computer nights, parents know and understand the teachers' goals, rationales, and practices prior to the conferences. They know about classroom learning projects. In this way, our uses of new technologies in the classroom have transformed the focus and purpose of these conferences, which have become a time to revisit what has been accomplished, talk about what learning challenges are being worked on, and plan the next educational steps.

The student-parent-teacher conferences start with portfolio presentations, which include presentations by students of how they use new technologies to learn. Then teachers and students share their assessments of student progress with the parents. (These discussions are familiar and safe for students because they are already used to meeting with their teacher during the school day to review scores and use assessments to plan next steps in learning.) Examples of student work produced with new technologies provide context in which to discuss the classroom environment, student accomplishments, and the assessment processes. The teacher uses the new technologies to demonstrate the next steps students will take in using these tools and provide examples of the kind of documents they will be creating. In setting next steps and goals, the focus is on discussing the learning plan for the classroom and what can be done at home. In our new traditions of student-parent-teacher collaboration, parents see that school is a place where the uses of new technologies aren't lagging behind how students use computers at home, but rather are helping to meet educational goals.

Protecting Privacy

In using new technologies, it is important and essential to honor the confidentiality of students. In our district, before any student uses the Internet in the classroom to conduct email communication, access websites for research, author classroom web pages, or participate in videoconferences, parents are informed of our classroom guidelines and procedures for protecting the confidentiality of students. In addition, parents and students must read and sign statements acknowledging the district's Internet-use policy and granting permission to post student work online, whether in writing, visual arts, digital images, or video. Furthermore, all discussions of student progress by teachers and parents should take place in face-to-face or private telephone conversations. They should not be communicated online except through password-protected online technologies.

Parents and Students Speak Out

Evidence of how new technologies are valued in building new traditions of student, parent, and teacher collaboration comes from parents in response to learning about schoolwork. One parent who had accessed the classroom web pages for the iEARN Water Habitat project with his child wrote:

> It's great that kids this age are learning to use digital images. Using the digital camera gives children a lot of confidence and it's a real hands-on experience. They can see how the computer tools help make the images. They can see the process and production of the pictures. They don't have to wait for film to be developed to use the pictures. The digital images are immediate. On a practical level the children can easily take the images from the camera into the computer and get right to their work and get their work

done. That justifies the technology right there! That wouldn't be possible without the technology. We can see that the children are really proud of their work!

Another parent responded to the student writing on the website by saying, "The children's pond writings are full of such vivid, realistic detail. . . . You can tell they got their descriptive words from a real experience."

When a parent talked about helping her student read the classroom website, she said, "The Water Habitat website design is nice. It's really user friendly for a child with the color choices and the big letters."

After one of our family computer nights, during which students showed their parents how we do email and website communication with global peers, a parent wrote:

I have seen firsthand the use of computer email and websites in the classroom. As the children write email messages to children around the world, they know they are writing to friends. This has resulted in a great enthusiasm for writing and has definitely enhanced the children's reading and writing skills. They are writing for a reason. The use of email messages and computer [has] brought the world into the classroom in a very real way.

At conference time, one student, who struggled with reading and often found schoolwork a challenge, couldn't wait to show her mom and dad how the class used the computer video editing tools to produce a video about one of our classroom projects. She showed the video to her parents and told them the steps of organizing the clips, giving the clips titles, writing the script, and recording the narration. Then she picked up a copy of the script and proudly read it straight through with accuracy. Watching and listening to her child, who was receiving both

Title I and Special Services support, the mom said, "I can't believe what she is able to do! She goes so fast with the computer. She knows exactly what she is doing and she can read the whole video script with expression. She can tell me tons of details about this project!"

When I see parents at school, talk to them on the phone, and communicate with them by email it is quite common for them to comment on specific classroom projects, such as the iEARN Comfort Quilt Project, which integrates visual arts, social studies, math and service learning. One parent said:

> My child has told me all about what the class is learning with the comfort quilts! He told me all about how the class made the squares, how they were sewn, and that the class sent them to children in Afghanistan and China. He showed me where these countries are. He read the comfort quilt website pages on the Internet to his dad and [me]. We even sent the website address to his grandparents so they could see what he was doing in school.

As parents follow the classroom work throughout the school year, they have reflective comments about the overall impact of new technologies on student learning. As one said:

> The "interaction factor" and immediacy of response offered by online access is great. It lets our children (and us) know that there really are a lot of people out there with similar interests— people who are willing to listen, discuss, and problem solve. What an asset technology is in terms of increasing understanding and communication for our children and generations to come.

Another parent added:

> For my son, iEARN and [the] Internet have expanded his understanding of children and places across the world. It is a wonder-

ful preparation for his future, because his future is tied in with computers. It also generates his interest in learning. It's given him a jumpstart for interest in education.

Evidence of how new technologies for learning are important to students is revealed in their comments about using these tools at school. First and second graders have these words to share:

> Email helps me make sense of my sentences. It makes me think about what I'm going to say. I like writing to people. Email helps me learn to read and write.

> I like the digital images because the pictures are realistic and you can put them into your writing right away. And you can brighten it and trim it to get just the picture you want and fix the size!

> On the computer you get to edit to make your writing better so other people can read your ideas. Editing is fun because it's easy to do on the computer. It would be hard to write everything down by hand because your hands get all sweaty holding the pencil and you need lots of paper because you have to copy everything over, and with a pencil you have to erase and sometimes the erasing doesn't work very well and the paper tears. When you have the computer, you can just delete and type again!

> I go to the library with my Dad and we can look at our pond websites there and I can practice my reading with him.

A second grader, when making a video presentation to iEARN teachers in Budapest, Hungary, decided to talk about how much she liked learning to read and write using email and how writing to teachers and children in other countries helped her learn: "I think all the children all over the world should have what they need to read and write like we have." She added, "And thanks to all the teachers around the world for helping us learn to read and write! We couldn't have done it without you!"

We now know, from just one short decade of use, how curricular new technologies can transform communication and collaborations in schools through global outreach to students and teachers worldwide and by reaching parents in our local community. New traditions of student, parent, and teacher collaboration with new technologies are transforming communication between school and home in ways not previously possible—in ways that powerfully support student learning.

For Further Information

Classroom iEARN Projects Website.
http://www.psd267.wednet.edu/~kfranz/iearn.html

Classroom Website by Students and Teacher Kristi Rennebohm Franz.
http://www.psd267.wednet.edu/~kfranz
Examples of Classroom Email Communication:
      http://www.psd267.wednet.edu/~kfranz/SchoolYear0102/Science0102/
        Whaleso0102/oceans.html
      http://www.psd267.wednet.edu/~kfranz/SocialStudies/
        socialstudies200001/gapcaring/sescaringart.html
      http://www.psd267.wednet.edu/%7Ekfranz/SocialStudies/
        socialstudies200001/iearncaring.html

GLOBE Project (Global Learning and Observation to Benefit the Environment).
http://www.globe.gov/globe_flash.html

International Education and Resource Network (iEARN).
http://www.iearn.org

Peace Corps World Wise Schools Programs.
http://www.peacecorps.gov/wws/

Rennebohm Franz, K. (2000a). Teaching for Understanding Picture of Practice: iEARN Water Habitat Project.
http://learnweb.harvard.edu/ent/gallery/pop3/pop3_1.cfm

Rennebohm Franz, K. (2000b). The Pedagogical Practice behind the Technology in a Primary Classroom.
http://www.ncrel.org/engauge/framewk/efp/research/efpressu.htm

Rennebohm Franz, K. (2000c). Literacy Learning through Technology: Primary Classroom.
http://www.ncrel.org/engauge/framewk/efp/environ/efpenvsu.htm

Rennebohm Franz, K. (2000d). There's a Lot of Learning Going On— Use Multiple Assessments to Capture IT All.
http://www.ncrel.org/engauge/framewk/efp/align/efpalisu.htm

Rennebohm Franz, K. (2000e). WRITE to Care Literacy Curriculum.
http://www.iearn.org/write

Rennebohm Franz, K. (2000f). Classroom Writing Process Curriculum.
http://www.psd267.wednet.edu/~kfranz/Literacy/birdprintwriting.htm

Rennebohm Franz, K. (2000g). Classroom Teacher Page.
http://www.psd267.wednet.edu/~kfranz/rennebohmfranz/
rennebohmfranz.htm

Don't Make Me Think! I'm Trying to Teach: Designing Web Environments That Enrich Teachers' Work

By James Moore

A tool is considered well designed for a task when it has two primary characteristics—ease of use and a perceived benefit for the user to accomplish the job at hand. This is true of any tool, whether it is a hammer for driving nails, an automobile for traveling a great distance, or a word processing application for typing this chapter. Sometimes an object's benefit and manner of use are readily apparent within a context, such as finding a bucket near a river when you need to retrieve water. Other times it requires a demonstration before one can grasp the best use of the object or understand its benefit. In either case, once a well-designed tool becomes familiar, the user seldom has to think about it when using it for an appropriate task.

In recent years, web-based environments increasingly have become viewed as potentially valuable tools for teaching, particularly in the classroom. However, a difficult challenge for instructional designers is designing web environments that convey both an ease of use and a clear benefit to teachers. The task of teaching is itself complex and differs from teacher to teacher, depending on his or her view of how people learn. Ideally, any tool designed to support or enrich the practice of teaching should be inherently flexible, accessible, and, when possible, customizable. Of course, limited resources and time make this impossible. Teachers wanting to leverage the Internet in their classrooms are often faced with web environments that are either generalized to a mass audience or assume a pedagogical approach that does not match their own.

Years ago, back in the technological stone age known as the early 1990s, we didn't use the term web *environment*. Web pages were simple text-only documents linked together via hypertext. Complexity was measured by the number of hyperlinks to different web pages hosted by an organization. Multipaged webs were denoted by terms like web*site* or, at most, *intranet*. Today, with online communities, 3-D worlds, and graphical interfaces with more design features than a museum by Frank Gehry, the term *environment* actually has begun to feel insufficient.

If I sound as though I yearn for those simpler days, I don't. Advances in Internet-based technologies promise dramatic changes in the way we learn and teach, as well as the way we interact as a society. Many of these changes are already taking place. In education, most students have access to Internet-based resources of some form and the number of web-based distance education programs increases every day (Mason, 1998). New developments in the Internet are bringing the Web into an important and new stage for educational use. Whereas the Web was previously viewed primarily as a resource for information-gathering and transactions, the increase of bandwidth and access has given rise to new technologies that stress the role of people online and allow interactivity among them.

However, I do sometimes yearn for the straightforward understanding and expectations we had of websites for teaching in the Internet's infancy and the practical design strategies that thrived during this period. As a teaching tool, the web offered access to content only in a digital format, much of it previously unavailable to most of us. Access was the clear benefit for use in the classroom. Ease of use mostly depended on whether the web designer placed hyperlinks in a clear and visible manner.

Today many web-based environments designed for education offer a wide range of activities and interactive features, from streaming video to role-playing games. As teaching tools they are complex, and each environment offers either a unique set of teaching opportunities or packages the same old opportunities differently. Ironically, as educational web environments have grown in sophistication, our ability to perceive their direct benefit to our teaching seems to have decreased. It has become more difficult to map the tool onto a specific task.

Many teachers I speak with point out that they are often unable to use many web environments in their teaching, even those designed for education, because constraints on their time and resources limit their ability to figure out how to use the many features of the site effectively. "I don't want to think about a whole new interface each time I use a new website in my teaching" is a common remark. Others observe that even many educationally sound web environments don't provide sufficient flexibility to be used with their approach to teaching, or don't support the schedule of classroom teachers. "How can I use an online lesson-planning tool that requires three hours to complete when I only have an hour each day for writing lessons?"

A critical problem in the design of many educational web environments is what I call the educational-use paradox. The environment's designer needs to assume that teachers will use the web environment in the same manner as they do any commercial web environment, that is, from the standpoint of usability. The environment should adhere to design conventions such as standard navigation schemes or the use of terms such as *home* for the home page. At the same time, the design needs to assume that teachers will use the web environment in a completely different manner than they do commercial ones. Using content to teach effectively is much different than deciding whether to purchase a book, and it requires a unique set of tasks.

If the task at hand is teaching, which characteristics have the greatest potential for making a web environment a tool that will enrich the work of teachers? There are ten that I have found to be essential in supporting the work of teachers in the classroom. I've chosen to discuss characteristics as opposed to specific features for two reasons. First, no matter how great the educational potential of a feature (e.g., an interactive bulletin board or game) may be, if it isn't embedded within an aptly designed environment, many teachers will not be able to use it effectively as a tool.

Second, I don't want to perpetuate a growing myth that increased interactive and complex features always equate to a stronger educational tool, or that a web environment must include these to be effective aids to learning. As tools for teaching, even basic presentational websites can only be effective classroom tools for teaching if they are designed correctly. The characteristics I discuss can be applied to any web environment, from the simplest text-based document to highly intricate online learning communities. Also, one can find many of these characteristics in content-rich websites that are not designed specially for educational use (e.g., general news sites), once one knows what to look for.

Of course, in the end it's the context in which web environments are used that determines the effectiveness of a design or feature. What is the specific task or goal? What is the setting in which it is used? Going back to the example I used earlier of the bucket near a river, the goal of retrieving water makes the bucket an obvious tool for transporting the water effectively. Without that goal, the bucket could as easily be used for a flower pot, or as a seat, if turned upside down. Although the specific goals and tasks of teaching vary a great deal from classroom to classroom, in general we are trying to create opportunities for learning. Just like the bucket, the use of a web environment can take many forms, depending on the current goal or task. The characteristics discussed below assume that the task is teaching and the goal is to help learners create meaning around a given topic or content piece.

1. Exploratory and guided approaches to content

One advantage we have with the inherent flexibility of digital media and hypertext is the ability to create multiple pathways to content easily and quickly. Hypertext allows us to move through content in either a linear or random fashion within a set of documents. Designers and content developers of educational web environments can leverage this flexibility to support different pedagogical approaches to content.

Hypertext is naturally supportive of exploratory approaches to learning, something that teachers have been exploiting since the Internet first entered the classroom. As a tool for teaching, hypertext also can be used to create more structured or guided pathways to content, to offer differing perspectives on the same piece of content, or to provide supports in helping learners make connections between disparate pieces of information. Examples of this include stepwise navigation structures that move a learner through content in a progressive manner; embedded prompts and other supports, such as a "pop-up" glossary and background information; or links to related materials.

Many web environments use hypertext in some or all of these ways. For example, general news sites often provide links to background or related articles and glossaries. However, to create effective tools for teaching, content developers for the web need to organize information in a manner that supports both exploratory and guided approaches. Web designers then need to structure and represent these approaches while considering the needs of classroom teachers. A good example of this is the "Windows to the Universe" website (http://www.windows.ucar.edu/frontPage/frontPage.htm) hosted by the University Corporation for Atmospheric Research (UCAR) at the University of Michigan. The designers of this website organized content on the solar system around central themes or topics in a flexible tutorial format. Using a semisequential structure, users have opportunities to explore links beyond the sequential presentation, which provides greater control over how one can approach the content.

2. Clear relationships to real classroom tasks

Web environments intended for classroom use must clearly outline what one can do within the site. It's not always clear how a web environment can be an effective classroom tool. The most common complaint I hear about using web environments for teaching is that teachers often have no idea what they can do once they get there. Either the features are scattered throughout the environment or it's unclear how the feature maps on to classroom tasks. A common design error for many tools, whether physical or virtual, is an assumption that the user will figure it out. Realistically, teachers typically do not have the time to search through a web environment for helpful features.

To create effective tools for teaching, web designers should consider creating a centralized list of the various tasks one can accomplish within a web environment. This needs to include task-oriented descriptions, as opposed to a list of labels. For example, having a link labeled "forum" informs us that a forum exists within the environment but gives no clue to how it might be used as a tool for teaching. Many educational web environments are creating "Action Lists," in which, in addition to "forum," one would see more active descriptions, such as "Create an online discussion." Another powerful and relatively simple solution is to create a page entitled "Using this web environment for teaching," where each area and feature would have suggestions or tips for using it in the classroom. The Geography Mentor Community (http://ngsmentor.org), hosted by the National Geographic Society's Education Foundation, provides several good examples. By using task charts, online tours, and guides under the "About this community" section, the designers of the Geography Mentor Community have made clear and explicit connections between what the environment offers and how it can be used to support the mentoring of new geography teachers.

3. Respect both for teachers' intellectual authority and for the integrity of content

A misconception I often see in the design of educational web environments is an assumption that the environment should be a fountain of expertise to which teachers come to drink. This misconception does not take into account the fact that teachers are the experts on classroom teaching, and it leads to web environments that are condescending at worst and stagnant at best. The best online resources for teachers tend to be web environments that include the thoughts and suggestions of other teachers. Online resource libraries that allow teachers to submit their own resources or to comment on a resource's usefulness significantly enrich the work of teachers by giving credibility and practical suggestions to each resource.

At the same time, a web environment is only useful if its content is perceived to be salient to a particular subject. Balancing the intellectual authority of teachers while maintaining the integrity of content can be achieved through a number of strategies. Examples include offering rating systems, requiring descriptions of submitted resources, and, most important, providing subject and grade level taught by the person who submitted each resource.

4. Helpful models of practice

Many tools require demonstrations of how others have used them before we can see how they might serve our own needs. This is especially true of web environments as tools for teaching because we have a short history of using the Internet in the classroom and we cannot assume all teachers are familiar with the medium. Web environments that contain examples of how teachers have used its content and various features in the classroom enable teachers to quickly discern whether or not a particular feature will help them meet a particular teaching goal. Models of practice also provide teachers with a clearer understanding of how a specific feature, such as an interactive game, works. For teachers new to the Internet, models can promote understanding of how the medium can be used as a tool in their teaching.

Examples of models of practice are as elaborate as case stories with video segments or as simple as text-based testimonials. The most effective models are those that provide some sort of context, such as type of school, size of district, grade level, and years of teaching experience.

5. Clear and appropriate development of content that "maps onto" subject matter

To be effective, a tool should be built with the appropriate material to handle the task for which it was designed. Glass, for example, would not be an appropriate material with which to make a hammer. As tools for teaching, web environments should be built with appropriate content that clearly reflects the subject matter at hand.

Generally speaking, there are three stages to the development of content for the Web. First, the content is arranged in appropriate sections based on the subject matter. Then the structure of the web environment is built to reflect the organized content. Finally, an interface is designed around the structure. If done well, each stage will reflect the intended subject matter while adhering to web standards and conventions. However, a common mistake among designers is to apply structures or interfaces that have nothing to do with the subject matter. Effective web environments for teaching typically communicate content organization and structure through its navigational elements. For example, a web environment on the subject of geography should reflect the basic categories for the field, thus allowing teachers to quickly access information they need. The Geography Mentor Community mentioned earlier (http://ngsmentor.org) developed a library categorized around standardized areas within the field of geography. This helps experienced teachers find what they need quickly while helping new teachers learn these categorizations as they use the environment's content.

6. Conceptual models rather than metaphors

In an effort to make a web environment more palatable or easier to use, many designers use metaphors to represent its content and features. Unfortunately, this often leads to an inappropriate organization or structure of content that, in the end, creates a barrier for the user. Teachers cannot use the features or content of a web environment effectively if they first have to learn (and re-learn) what's hidden behind a misguided metaphor. For example, a village metaphor probably will work well if the primary objective of the environment is to house an online community. But it might not work as well for a web environment supporting the teaching of math, even if a component of the environment has community-based features. A teacher trying to find lesson plans does not want to remember whether they are located within the "Town Hall" or "Community Center."

The debate over the use of metaphors in interface design is well documented (Nielsen, 2000; Norman, 1998; Preece, 1994). Web environments I have found to be effective tools for teaching usually are based on conceptual models more than metaphors. Conceptual models are more direct and easy to follow because they are based on the user's understanding of a domain or topic. They also use natural language and structures based on user expectations. A web environment supporting the teaching of math, for example, would be organized around the common language and categories expected by math teachers.

7. Opportunities for moving from the presentation of information toward the creation of meaning

Helping learners make connections between disparate pieces of information is a perpetual challenge in teaching. Web-based technologies offer new opportunities for teachers on this front, due to their potential for interactivity, linking pieces of information together via hypertext, and the relative ease with which information can be modified. Unlike traditional textbooks, the web allows us to move beyond the presentation of information toward opportunities for the creation of meaning alongside or embedded within a piece of content.

Of course, different learning goals call for different connections. By leveraging the flexibility and potential for interactivity in web-based technologies, designers can offer opportunities for teachers to add their own prompts, questions, or other supports to promote critical thinking around content. Current advances on the Internet are making it easier to create such opportunities via online bulletin boards, chat rooms, or customizable pages. To build more effective tools for teaching, web developers and designers must create more opportunities for teachers to guide their students through content based on their own learning goals. Web environments with individual online activities, such as Explore Science (http://www.explorescience.com/index.cfm), can provide teachers with a virtual toolbox of useful aids. By building a searchable, easy-to-use library of interactive activities, the developers at Explore Science offer teachers new opportunities to help their students create their own meaning around often abstract scientific concepts.

8. Different modes of experiencing information

Another advantage of the inherent flexibility of digital media, such as the web, is the opportunity for multiple representation of content to suit different learning styles or needs. Digital media offer access to content previously unavailable to many learners who may have difficulty with traditional text-based content (Rose & Meyer, 2002). However, the rise of highly graphical interfaces presents new challenges to learners with vision impairments or those who have difficulty processing graphical information.

To be effective tools for teaching, it is critical that web environments include multiple representations of content wherever possible.

Due to new legislation and a greater awareness of issues around universal access, web environments, particularly in the field of education, are following design standards to provide access to the greatest range of learners possible. Typically this takes the form of text-based alternatives to graphic elements within a web environment. In addition, beyond providing greater access to the content itself, teachers can also use multiple representations of content to support different learning styles. The Teaching Every Student Web environment at CAST (http://www. cast.org/teachingeverystudent) offers many examples of how text can be augmented with digital media to provide multiple representations of the same content.

9. A clear pedagogical framework and educational agenda

The importance of basing a web environment intended to support teaching on a pedagogical framework cannot be understated. This is what separates an educational environment from other types of web environments. By organizing, structuring, and representing the content of a web environment around an articulated framework, a designer can help transform a repository of information into a useful teaching tool. For example, the Education with New Technologies (ENT) web environment (http://learn.harvard.edu/ent) was designed to help teachers use new technologies in the classroom to support their use of the Teaching for Understanding framework (Wiske, 1998). The ENT web environment exemplifies and promotes Teaching for Understanding in the actual design of the environment by supporting the four elements of the framework: generative topics, understanding goals, performances of understanding, and ongoing assessment.

In addition, it's important that the designer/developer understand the larger educational agenda on which the environment is built. Many web environments have characteristics that support teachers' practice, but I have found that those with a clear educational agenda are the most effective in enriching a teacher's work. I use the term *agenda* because there is a wide range of assumptions about the place of technology in teaching, views on how people learn, and other social factors that play into the design and development of any tool built to support teaching. Even if a clear pedagogical framework is articulated within a web environment, these other factors often are not.

Web environments in which the developers and designers have articulated a fuller educational agenda usually provide a greater number of features that support more meaningful learning. For instance, many web environments state an affinity for constructionist theories of learning, yet offer only presentational modes of content. By articulating a fuller educational agenda, designers are better equipped to see discrepancies between the tenets of a pedagogical framework and the actual presentation of content.

10. Content, content, content

In the end it all comes down to the content. I have seen numerous web environments in which the developers have addressed many or most of the characteristics mentioned above and short-changed content development. Without solid, reliable content, educational web environments become like many cable channels, where once you pause for a moment you realize there's nothing of substance to hold you.

Design strategies that are attentive to content lead to web environments in which navigation structures, page layout, and graphics enhance pertinent information rather than diminishing it. Additionally, emphasizing content keeps designers conscious of the need to provide quick and easy access to it for teachers. Many developers want teachers to linger on their web environment, but the reality is that most teachers don't have the time and prefer to find salient content, download or print, and move on. What keeps teachers coming back most often is the ability to find reliable content.

Of course there are many other characteristics that make web environments a good tool for teaching—social interactivity, opportunities for professional development, access to teaching materials, and class management are just a few. The ten characteristics discussed here are the ones I have found applicable to the greatest range of web environments and, typically, they are the easiest to implement. They also focus on content, something many teachers will tell you is most beneficial to their practice. Ultimately, a web environment is a well-designed tool for teaching if it supports ease of use around content, and enhances its benefits by providing new teaching opportunities.

References

Mason, R. (1998). *Globalizing education: Trends and applications.* New York: Routledge.

Nielsen, J. (2000). *Designing web usability.* Indianapolis: New Riders.

Norman, D. A. (1998). *The invisible computer: Why good products can fail, the personal computer is so complex, and information appliances are the solution.* Cambridge, MA: MIT Press.

Preece, J. (1994). *Human-computer interaction.* Reading, MA: Addison-Wesley.

Rose, D., & Meyer, A. (with Strangman, N., & Rappolt, G.). (2002). *Teaching every student in the digital age: Universal design for learning.* Alexandria, VA: Association for Supervision and Curriculum Development.

Wiske, M. S. (Ed.). (1998). *Teaching for understanding: Linking research with practice.* San Francisco: Jossey-Bass.

Curriculum Access in the Digital Age

By David T. Gordon

In a school north of Boston, a dozen seventh graders are enjoying a novel experience: They are reading a book from the district's required reading list, the same book that their peers have been assigned. *Hatchet*, written by Newbery-award winner Gary Paulsen, is an adventure story about a young man's two-month survival in the Canadian wilderness following a plane crash. Most of the students have learning disabilities, so they relate well to Brian, the protagonist, because they too have felt lost in the woods—when trying to read books written for kids their age.

They sit at computers, each wearing headphones, and read a digital text of *Hatchet* using a program called Thinking Reader. For some, the computer simultaneously highlights each word on the screen and reads it aloud. Students who don't understand a particular word can get a definition with a click of the mouse.

Occasionally, a cartoon genie appears on screen and prompts them to stop and think more deeply about the text. It may ask them to summarize what they've read, predict what happens next, formulate the kinds of questions teachers might ask, and seek to clarify confusing passages. If they forget what those strategies entail, the genie offers hints. The students type their responses into a box at the bottom of the screen—a journal that will later help them and their teacher assess their progress. The teacher moves among the children, answering questions the genie can't and prompting them further—to be more specific in their responses, perhaps, or to consider another point of view. The class will eventually gather off line to discuss the book with their teacher; they do this about once every two weeks.

Thinking Reader employs elements of Reciprocal Teaching, an instructional method for teaching reading comprehension developed by reading specialists Annemarie Palincsar and Ann Brown in the 1980s. The idea is to get students to be active readers using a four-part strategy: formulate questions, summarize, clarify, and predict. In one-on-one or group sessions, teachers and students take turns leading a discussion about the text. Although the method requires considerable time to master from both teachers and students, research shows that it can lead to dramatic improvement in the performance of poor readers.

Still, it's labor intensive for teachers, and students in a traditional reading class can be inadvertently left out of the class discussions, especially in a large class. Technology makes it possible for each student to directly engage the text through prompts embedded in the story itself and various decoding supports—supplemented, of course, by interactions with the teacher, who spends his or her classroom time monitoring student progress and providing targeted guidance to individual students.

New Expectations

Why is access to age-appropriate books from the general curriculum so important? For one thing, researchers say, such books are interesting to students and relevant to their lives, which are key to motivation. Also, those who are excluded from the general curriculum because of disabilities have less in common with their peers, which constitutes a blow to self-esteem. Then there's the law. Under the 1997 Individuals with Disabilities Education Act (IDEA) reauthorization, special education students must be given a fair opportunity to learn what their mainstream peers do in the general curriculum. Schools are expected to accommodate students' individual needs so that they can progress at a pace that is cognitively challenging to them. Also, many state standards ask schools to improve learning outcomes for all students, including those with special needs. To accomplish this, such students need fresh methods of engaging and responding to the curriculum.

Even before the 1997 IDEA amendments, researchers at the Center for Applied Special Technology (CAST)—where Thinking Reader was developed—anticipated this change in thinking. Cofounders Anne Meyer and David Rose started CAST in 1984 to explore the use of technology for students with disabilities. By the early 1990s, they realized that, rather than finding ways to use technology to help students work with inaccessible materials (such as books), the materials themselves, as well as the curricula they supported, had to be reconsidered.

Meyer and Rose began using the term *Universal Design for Learning* (UDL) to describe their work. The term *universal design* comes from the fields of architecture and product design, where it refers to built-in accommodations, such as ramps, sidewalk curb cuts, and automatic doors, that benefit users of all abilities. The CAST team began thinking about K–12 curricula in a similar way. In any classroom, the abilities and learning styles of students can vary widely. If such differences are not considered and accommodated, can we really say all students have equal access to the curriculum? Thus the idea of UDL began to take shape, a model in which the diverse needs and abilities of students are met by providing them with a variety of ways to learn what they need to know, demonstrate that understanding, and be assessed.

"UDL is about expanding the number of opportunities kids have to succeed," says Rose, who also teaches in the Technology in Education Program at the Harvard Graduate School of Education. "It can be a daunting prospect for schools because it doesn't just say every child needs to do well—everyone agrees with that—but that we need to broaden our thinking about what success is and how we measure it."

In their writings, Rose and Meyer (2002) point to recent brain research to bolster their argument for multiple approaches to teaching and learning. They note that neurologists such as Richard Cytowic have identified three distinct but interrelated brain networks at work in every learner. Glucose—the sugar that fuels the brain—burns at varying intensity in the front, middle, and back of the brain, depending on which system is being taxed the most. The *recognition* network identifies certain patterns (letters, words, sounds, objects), the *strategic* network generates patterns such as plans and actions (spelling words, playing a trumpet, solving an algebra problem in sequential steps), and the *affective* system produces a feeling response to those patterns (pleasure at hearing a tuba, boredom in writing essays, excitement about a novel) and therefore has a lot to do with stoking or dampening motivation.

Because of this, write Rose and Meyer, a particular lesson or classroom task will challenge students in different ways. If, for example, a group reading assignment aims to improve comprehension skills (the strategic system), what happens to the student with low vision who wears herself out just trying to decipher the words on the page (the recognition system)? She gets discouraged and certainly can't benefit from the lesson on comprehension strategies. Why not provide additional help decoding, at least for the moment, so she too can focus on comprehension?

Most schools can't accommodate multiple styles because they rely almost exclusively on print media. In testimony before the U.S. Senate Appropriations Committee about the future of educational technology, Rose explained his vision:

> In print versions the content is dried into the paper, and its display is fixed, immutable, "one size fits all." In digital versions, on the other hand, content is presented dynamically on a computer screen. As a result, the power of the computer can be used to display the content in ways that are highly variable, malleable . . . [D]igital versions of traditional curricular materials can effectively reduce barriers to learning and reduce the costs associated with more expensive adaptations and pull-out programs.

Because the words of a traditional book are fixed on the page, they cannot be easily adapted for use by students who can't otherwise read them. Digital text is far more flexible and, with the right computer programs, can give students access to materials that otherwise would require expensive and time-consuming adaptations. For example, to aid a student with low vision, a teacher could spend hours making large-sized photocopies of textbook pages. With digital text, the student could simply increase the font size to suit her need or use the text-to-speech function to listen to the text being read.

Promising Results

CAST recently wrapped up an evaluation of Thinking Reader funded by the U.S. Department of Education's Office of Special Education Programs. More than 100 students reading in the lower 25th percentile read books like *Hatchet* and Yoko Ka Watkins' *So Far From the Bamboo Grove*. Sixty-three students read a digital version on computer, while a control group of 39 used traditional books and engaged in regular small-group and class discussions using Reciprocal Teaching. All 102 students took the Gates MacGinitie reading assessment—a paper-and-pencil standardized test—before and after the seven-month instructional period.

The results were promising, says CAST's chief education officer Bridget Dalton. After controlling for gender and pretest reading scores, those who used Thinking Reader gained, on average, approximately a half-year in grade level in reading comprehension; those in the control group averaged only slight gains. The half-year's improvement was a notable achievement for kids whose reading had not improved very much from year to year.

Beyond the standardized test, other assessments revealed some advantages of Thinking Reader. Measurements of "time on task" showed that students using traditional texts were more likely to lose their focus and become distracted. Those using Thinking Reader did not get as much time in group discussion as those in traditional reading classes, but they did have more opportunity to dig into the text and try to make meaning of it than their counterparts, who could drift out of group conversations or get distracted by other struggling readers. Says Dalton: "Students who were on the computer managed to stay glued to the text for long stretches. Some of them had never demonstrated such concentration before."

Interviews with students and classroom observations suggest that Thinking Reader gave students a sense that they were in charge of the learning process and understood what strategies could help them make sense of their reading. Interviews also suggested that reading the same books as their peers both encouraged and motivated them. "So many have been shut out of reading engaging literature because of their reading difficulties," says Dalton. "Access to good, age-appropriate books helped them buy into the work of reading and responding."

CAST researchers are reluctant to draw too many conclusions from this initial study. Indeed, like a lot of education research, it may raise more questions than it answers. For instance, why did some children make little progress using Thinking Reader? Was technology in their particular cases actually a hindrance? Why did some students make dramatically more progress using the computer than the group's average gain? Why did girls in both groups outperform boys on the final standardized tests? Did the fact that Thinking Reader is a new, exciting product affect the outcomes—and would children still show improvement a few years down the line, once the novelty wore off?

Although questions remain, the research has contributed to a small but growing body of research demonstrating the benefits of digital texts that have helpful, built-in resources such as changeable fonts, glossaries, concept maps, multimedia tools (video, sound), illustrations, tutorial aids, and e-notebooks. These resources are showing positive effects on students' achievement and motivation among special needs and general education populations alike.

If universally designed innovations such as Thinking Reader are to take root, giving all students access to the general education curriculum, one thing will certainly have to change: the way information is presented in the classroom. For that reason, CAST has formed the National Center on Accessing the General Curriculum (NCAC), a collaboration with the federal Office of Special Education Programs, the Council for Exceptional Children, Harvard Law School, Boston College, and the Minnesota-based Parents Advocacy Center for Educational Rights. NCAC is working to increase awareness of the benefits of flexible, digital curricular materials and to provide an online depository of such materials, called the Universal Learning Center. The resources will be offered in a variety of formats and include search capabilities so that educators, parents, and students can access them with ease.

Such a resource would be welcomed in districts like Concord, New Hampshire, where teachers and parent-volunteers scan textbook pages into computers to make them accessible to students with disabilities. "It's time consuming and requires constant upkeep to scan your own materials," says Donna Palley, special education coordinator at Concord High School. "Somebody's always having to wait for another chapter to be scanned."

William Henderson, principal of the Patrick J. O'Hearn Elementary School in Boston, has a similar hope. "I'd like to have [an online] library where we could get not only books but also creative lesson plans—redesigned for those with all kinds of disabilities," says Henderson, whose diverse, inclusive school of 220 serves more than 50 special needs students. "That would enable teachers to spend more time teaching and less time adapting lessons to individual kids."

The Publishing Challenge

The real challenge will be to get the cooperation of publishing houses, which are skittish about licensing digital materials. The availability of flexible, digital textbooks and curricular materials is key to any sustained effort to provide students of all abilities with the same educational opportunities. But as the widely reported case of Napster shows, digital material is easily pirated and bootlegged. Publishing houses want to ward off the headaches brought on by unauthorized distribution of copyrighted material that have plagued the film and music industries.

Federal law permits "the blind or other persons with disabilities" or organizations working on their behalf to reproduce copyrighted books in accessible media, such as Braille and cassette tapes. However, the law is also ambiguous: Are those with dyslexia, learning disabilities, or physical conditions that make the use of books difficult considered "persons with disabilities"? Without a clear definition, some advocates of those with special needs are reluctant to use copyrighted material for what they think are legitimate purposes and risk lawsuits from publishers.

Other legal dilemmas include the fact that many publishing contracts don't spell out who has rights to digital material at all. Authors' advocates say that if the contract is not clear, then authors retain those rights—and publishers can't grant permissions for digital content even if they want to. Gradually, that issue may atrophy as more and more contracts include specific language on digital rights.

"The technology is just about there to open up worlds of curricula to disabled children, but these legal issues may stand in the way," says Harvard Law School Professor Martha L. Minow, whose work includes analysis of the implementation of state and federal laws protecting students with disabilities.

For publishers, digital-rights management is just one sticky issue, says Stephen Driesler, executive director of the Association of American Publishers' school division. Another challenge is that publishers are under pressure to make significant changes to their production processes. It won't happen overnight. The basic source files publishers produce—that is, what actually gets sent to the printer—are not typically created in programs that favor accessibility, says Driesler. Since textbooks are filled with illustrations such as photos and charts, turning them into easily readable documents is no simple task. That should change once publishers switch to using the highly flexible XML language. "It'll probably be three to five years before XML is in widespread use in the industry, but it's coming," says Driesler. "And it will definitely make accessibility much easier."

The biggest question publishers have about e-publishing is what business model will prove to be viable when or if electronic books make significant inroads into the market for traditional paper books. Will books be offered on a subscription, pay-per-use, or some other basis? Driesler says there's no consensus among publishers about what that model will look like. "But I do know a lot of people are working very hard to try and figure it out," he says.

*   *   *

To some, the promises of UDL and programs like Thinking Reader may sound Pollyannaish, especially when the resources needed for such innovations are scarce in many schools. Without enough of the right equipment or the right training, technology's leverage is lost. Yet as the work of CAST and a number of organizations with similar missions demonstrates, digital technologies can be powerful tools in the hands of teachers who use proven, research-based teaching strategies; have high-quality professional development; and obtain the support of administrators who are committed to finding fresh approaches to meet the needs of all students.

This article was originally published in the Harvard Education Letter *(January/ February 2002 issue).*

For Further Information

Dolan, R. P., & Hall, T. E. (2001). Universal design for learning: Implications for large-scale assessment." *IDA Perspectives, 27*(4), 22–25.

Kelly, K. (2000). New independence for special-needs kids. In D. T. Gordon (Ed.), *The digital classroom: How technology is changing the way we teach and learn* (pp. 36–48). Cambridge, MA: Harvard Education Letter.

Meyer, A., & Rose, D. H. (1998). *Learning to read in the computer age*. Cambridge, MA: Brookline Books.

O'Neill, L. M. (2001, June). Thinking readers: Helping students take charge of their learning. *Exceptional Parent, 31*(6), 32–33.

Orkwis, R. (1999). *Curriculum access and universal design for learning* (Special report of ERIC Clearinghouse on Disabilities and Gifted Education). Reston, VA: Council on Exceptional Children.

Rose, D. H. (2001, July 25). Testimony before the U.S. Senate Appropriations Committee. Available online at http://jset.unlv.edu/16.4/asseds/rose.html

Rose, D. H., & Meyer, A. (with Strangman, N., & Rappolt, G.). (2002). *Teaching every student in the digital age: Universal design for learning*. Alexandria, VA: Association for Supervision and Curriculum Development.

Making the Most of What's Available

Although the term *Universal Design for Learning* (UDL) was coined at CAST, a number of other research and service organizations are also working to make curriculum materials, tools, and activities more accessible for students of all abilities, including these:

Alliance for Technology Access is a network of community organizations dedicated to helping children and adults with disabilities increase their use of technology tools. Contact: 2175 E. Francisco Blvd., Suite L, San Rafael, CA 94901; tel: 415-455-4575; fax: 415-455-0654; TTY: 415-455-0491; email: atainfo@ataaccess.org. **www.ataccess.org**

Bookshare.org, a project of the nonprofit organization Benetech, provides an online archive of books for those with visual impairments and other "print" disabilities. The archive is being built in part by school practitioners sharing scanned-in material. **www.bookshare.org**

In addition to research and product development, **CAST** (formerly the Center for Applied Special Technology) offers professional development courses and publications about implementing Universal Design for Learning. Contact: 40 Harvard Mills Sq., Suite 3, Wakefield, MA 01880-3233; tel: 781-245-2212; fax: 781-245-5212. **www.cast.org**

The **Council for Exceptional Children** is a professional development and advocacy organization dedicated to improving education for students of all abilities, including those with disabilities. It's also a great information resource and runs the federally sponsored ERIC Clearinghouse on Disabilities and Gifted Education (http://ericec.org). Contact: 1110 North Globe Rd., Suite 300, Arlington, VA 22201; tel: 703-620-3660; fax: 703-264-9494; TTY: 703-264-9446; email: service@cec.sped.org. **www. cec.sped.org**

Education Development Center, Inc. devoted the summer 2000 issue of its journal *Mosaic* to inclusive practices, including UDL. It can be viewed on the web at **www.edc.org/spotlight/mos_ format/spec_ed/intro.htm** Contact: 55 Chapel St., Newton, MA 02458-1060; tel: 617-969-7100. **www.edc.org**

The **Office of Special Education Programs** of the U.S. Department of Education provides leadership and grants to help states and local school districts better serve children with disabilities, particularly through the implementation of the Individuals with Disabilities Education Act (IDEA). It also funds and publishes relevant research. Contact: Office of Special Education Programs, U.S. Department of Education, 400 Maryland Ave., S.W.,Washington, DC 20202; tel: 202-205-5507. **www.ed.gov/ offices/OSERS/OSEP/**

The **Parent Advocacy Coalition for Educational Rights (PACER)** sponsors programs to expand opportunities for children with disabilities. Contact: 8161 Normandale Blvd., Minneapolis, MN 55437; tel: 952-838-9000; fax: 952-838-0199; TTY: 952-838-0190; email: pacer@pacer.org. **www.pacer.org**

Online Distance Learning: Is It Worth the Cost and Effort?

By Louise Grace Yarnall

In the 1990s, the innovation of offering distance learning via the Internet quickly found a natural constituency among working adults seeking to obtain their high school diplomas or college degrees. The approach had appeal because of the obvious conveniences offered by the technology, such as flexible scheduling and no commuting. More than 11 percent of the 14.6 million students attending two- and four-year institutions were taking online courses by the end of the decade.

At the K–12 level, distance learning has had a far less noticeable impact: Only 0.001 percent (or about 50,000) of the estimated 47.5 million K–12 public school students were expected to enroll in an online course nationwide in the 2001–2002 school year, despite the fact that tens of millions of dollars have been invested in such programs since the mid-1990s. By comparison, the charter school and homeschooling movements have had a far greater impact: Five times as many students attend charter schools as take part in online learning, and 17 times as many are homeschooled. These miniscule enrollment figures coupled with the high costs reflect the challenges of providing online distance learning to K–12 students. They also raise questions about the ultimate value to society of this grand experiment.

Is online distance learning at the K–12 level worth the cost and effort? Before addressing that question, let's consider who uses such services. School districts and businesses have discovered many possible constituencies for such programs: homeschooled students, Advanced Placement students, at-risk students, and students seeking quality and flexibility in their public school experience. The specific reasons for choosing to learn on line are as varied as the students themselves. Homeschooling families often seek support for challenging subjects. Some at-risk students who find it difficult to conform to a traditional school environment prefer the more independent context of an online class. Some families go on line because they are displeased with the offerings or safety at their local schools, while others have young people juggling complicated schedules that limit their ability to attend school consistently each day. Some students face health problems, such as asthma or chronic illness, that limit their ability to attend regular school.

To meet the demands of these different K–12 interest groups, pioneers in the online education field have found a variety of ways to sponsor and maintain their programs. Some have focused on financing through traditional institutions, such as state departments of education, state universities and colleges, local school boards, and regional offices of education. One pioneer, the Virtual High School (VHS; http://www.govhs.org), created a whole new approach, dubbed the consortium model, in which member schools each get a certain number of free spots in online courses in exchange for each teacher who creates and offers an online course based at the school.

Some of the large-scale government grants that supported the early pioneers represented one-time research and development expenditures of the type that launch all great societal innovations. Others have adopted some newer institutional structures for financing, such as charter schools. In the case of charter schools, funding is achieved by diverting money from traditional school programs. This shifting of resources raises important questions about whether such efforts hurt or benefit existing schools as public attention and dollars flow to online efforts.

Along the way, the pioneers have encountered a similar set of challenges. They have navigated steep regulatory and political hurdles, covered exorbitant start-up costs, and educated students and teachers on how to learn and teach in a new way. My colleagues Robert Kozma, Andrew Zucker, and Camille Marder and I reviewed many of these challenges in depth in our book on the most prominent consortium model of K–12 distance learning, *The Virtual High School*. We found that the K–12 distance learning movement holds great promise for a small, committed segment of students, but remains overshadowed by long-term questions about its fiscal sustainability. I review some cases of pioneers who have grappled with the most difficult challenges and remained committed to distance learning at this level.

Lessons from VHS: The Challenge of Building a High-Quality Program

Needless to say, online classes provide a very different experience for both teachers and students than traditional classes do, requiring both to employ a different set of skills. Among the K–12 pioneers, the VHS has had one of the most public trial-and-error experiences learning about the kinds of course designs and management approaches that work. Founded in 1996 under a federal grant to the nonprofit Concord Consortium and the Hudson, Massachusetts, public schools, VHS operates according to a consortium model, in which teachers from schools across the United States design and run their own online courses. This model provides an interesting petri dish showing the many possible variations in course design and teaching. As a condition of its federal grant, VHS was required to engage in an evaluation handled by my employer, SRI International, a research and policy institute in Menlo Park, California.

In the broadest terms, VHS learned that getting K–12 distance learning to work requires two basic ingredients: the right rationale and the right student learning experience. The rationale hinges on a clear vision of the students served. States recently entering the K–12 online learning field tend to state their goals early and often on websites. They talk about the kinds of students they seek to serve, and they keep track of the students' needs through periodic surveys. VHS, for example, focused on offering a variety of courses and regularly tracked student reports on course quality. Courses were dropped or changed according to this feedback. VHS also learned about its core demographic through this process. Typically, VHS appealed to affluent, white, college-bound juniors and seniors seeking unique elective courses. Only 17 percent were economically disadvantaged and only 20 percent were minority students. Nearly all spoke English fluently (Zucker, Kozma, Yarnall, & Marder, 2003).

Achieving the right learning experience involves careful analysis of all online features and interactions. A wide range of courses is ready for use today through various online providers, but that does not mean that these course offerings are plug-and-play. In developing an online learning program, the key decisionmakers—local education agencies, teachers, and parents—need to review the existing courses and see if the overall design meets their needs. Course formats range from low service to high service. On the low-service end, the course may amount to little more than an email correspondence course, in which the students receive lots of print materials in the mail and email their work to a distant teacher. On the high-service end, courses involve options for both asynchronous and synchronous teacher-led learning, where students work together in virtual classes and engage in chats, threaded discussions, collaborative white-board projects, and even streaming video activities.

Good teacher-student communication is a primary ingredient for success in any class. This goal is particularly difficult to achieve in an online setting, where there is no face-to-face interaction. In the virtual learning environment, students can be in different time zones from their teachers, making access at all times through voicemail highly practical. To encourage frequent communication across time zones, the Florida Virtual School (http://www.flvs.net) provides students with a 24-hour telephone number and a guarantee that teachers will respond to student calls promptly. An expert panel assembled by SRI to evaluate VHS courses outlined other key standards relating to course content, pedagogy, design, and assessment.

Courses receiving higher ratings by panelists (and students) encouraged active interaction that involved more than completing assignments and emailing them. Teachers provided timely and regular feedback and used their voices skillfully to foster student discussion and debate. One VHS teacher commented that asking students to complete "a lot of small assignments" rather than a few large ones helped maintain a consistent level of student engagement in the course (Zucker et al., 2003, p. 108). In addition, expectations about course objectives and attendance were clearly stated and enforced. Multiple methods of instruction were used—reading, discussion, teamwork, simulation, laboratories, assigned writing, critiques, peer review, and presentations.

Grades were based on multiple indicators and often included students' self-assessments.

Another important point to consider when determining what courses might work well on line focuses on finding a good match between subject and online medium. The key is not so much selecting a particular type of course, but crafting its content in a way that exploits the strengths and minimizes the weaknesses of the online medium. The VHS course catalog covered a range of topics, from mathematics, literature, science, and social studies, to film appreciation, aviation, art history, musical composition, and web design. This range suggests that nearly any topic can succeed if structured well within the medium. A comparison of face-to-face and online versions of the same courses suggested that online students reported engaging in less communication with their classmates and teacher than those in face-to-face environments. That posed a particular challenge for participants in a photography course, where high-quality discussion and critique was expected. In this case, part of the problem was technological: Asynchronous communication prevented students from engaging in real give and take, and students had to make comments on a blank screen *after* viewing the photograph rather than making the comments *while* viewing a photograph.

Many teachers found that designing online courses can be more time intensive than designing traditional courses. Their online course design work often involved identifying relevant readings on the Internet, which required searching for the best websites and materials. It also involved creating online documents to support course participation—from reading lists to online spaces for threaded discussion. "It's not like a regular course with a textbook where you just have to assign reading," said teacher Cynthia Costilla, who estimated that she devoted two to two-and-a-half hours to post new units to her course (Zucker et al., 2003). Also, courses requiring a high level of hands-on activity may require additional planning by the online teacher. For example, one pre-engineering teacher found it frustrating that in the online environment one could not "just show them" when students did not understand a procedure (p. 73).

In our evaluation of VHS, we found that not every teacher who is an inspired lecturer and performer in a regular classroom can facilitate online discussion well. Training is usually needed to build skills of facilitation, coaching, providing support, and fading away. The VHS designers outlined the basics in their book, *Facilitating Online Learning*, which summarizes the key ingredients of high-quality facilitation, such as reading all student postings, intervening only occasionally to provide strategic guidance, and maintaining the constructive tone of the conversation. Most VHS teachers (89%) reported that teaching and managing an online course required more time than a face-to-face course. Much of this time was devoted to learning more about technology. Eighty percent of teachers reported also learning some new teaching or assessment skills that they later used in their face-to-face classrooms.

From the beginning, VHS realized the importance of the teacher's role and instituted a teacher-training program. VHS chief executive officer Liz Pape has described the process of developing this 26-week online professional development course as "one of the most challenging aspects" of VHS. When the program began, the VHS central staff worked with only 20 to 30 teachers, and it was easy to monitor progress. In later years, when the number of teachers enrolled in training classes grew to more than 100, the monitoring process got more challenging. Additional VHS facilitators were brought in to provide feedback and maintain a ratio of one facilitator for every ten teachers.

Student selection appears to be particularly important at the K–12 level. Not all students can handle the independence an online learning model requires. Many online providers, such as VHS and the New Mexico Virtual School (http://www.intelligented.com/nmvs), now screen students by having them take a survey about their ability to study independently before they enroll. The VHS survey asks students whether they usually do their work on time, how much responsibility they take for their own learning, and how well they can read and write. Efforts to use online settings to achieve educational equity may be hampered when learners have limited linguistic skills. Many schools, such as VHS, require careful screening of students by third parties, such as school guidance counselors or teachers.

Student assessment is another area of particular concern at the K–12 level. In a context where the teacher can never see the students, success depends on maintaining a high level of integrity and honesty. In the evaluation of VHS, there was little mention of problems with student cheating. Teachers usually relied more on a portfolio of work collected over a long period of time rather than a one-time final exam. One course, for example, required students to fill out a weekly journal. When working in an online context, it is especially important to maintain a wide range of frequent assessments to ensure a more accurate portrayal of student progress. Some of the artifacts generated in an online environment offer a teacher new ways to assess student progress. For example, a teacher may review the written record of threaded discussions to assess different levels of student participation and understanding.

Other online distance-learning standards developed for the higher-ed market, such as the 24 benchmarks identified by the Institute for Higher Education, provide some solid guidelines for the K–12 online provider, teacher, or parent. These benchmarks, which have earned the endorsement of the National Education Association, focus on a range of issues from the delivery platform quality to student learning outcomes. In summary, they recommend:

- electronic security and a reliable, centralized delivery system
- standards for courses and periodic reviews of instructional materials to ensure they are engaging and high level
- frequent interaction between teachers and students with timely feedback
- clear presentation of course objectives and careful selection of students who demonstrate the ability to work independently
- various forms of support for students on admissions, tuition and fees, research resources, and convenient access to technical support staff
- adequate forms of faculty support, such as teacher training and troubleshooting resources
- regular assessment of teaching and learning and data collection on enrollment, costs, and technology use

Political Challenges: The Special Case of Cyber Charters

Beyond the details of how to operate an online learning program, local educators also need to consider the impact of offering an online program in their communities. As some pioneers in Pennsylvania found, the development of any online learning program is likely to bring out a host of critics who will argue that public resources would be better spent on improving existing schools. This is especially true when online programs are meant to replace, rather than supplement, regular schools. The result can be some fierce political battles. The case of cyber charter schools is one good example.

At the K–12 level, proponents of online distance learning have often aligned with the school choice movement. In Pennsylvania, for example, the emergence of seven online K–12 distance learning charter schools occurred within three years of the passage of the state's charter school law. These cyber charters quickly generated political heat. Although the students attending these schools accounted for less than one percent of the state's public school enrollment, the students collectively represented about $1.2 million in state funding. This was a mere fraction of state funding for education, but it was shifted overnight from their home districts to the new cyber charters. School board members across the state were stunned to receive tuition bills for thousands of dollars from one particular cyber school, sometimes just after they approved their annual budgets. Several districts refused to pay, thereby prompting the state to withhold funding to the protesting districts. Up to 23 districts sued, and the state teachers' union sided with the districts.

The online school at the center of the controversy, the Western Pennsylvania Cyber Charter School (http://www.wpccs.com), began modestly in Midland, a tiny community devastated by the collapse of the steel industry. In 1986, the Midland Borough School District shut down its only high school, forcing local students to commute to high schools in Ohio and neighboring districts. In 2000, the district opened the cyber school to permit 500 local high school students who lived in the area to complete their studies locally. Although the school did not seek publicity or market its program, word spread, and, by its second year, 996 students from as many as 196 other Pennsylvania districts had enrolled in online courses.

The controversy put the debate about costs and benefits in sharp focus. On one hand, traditional schools saw their budgets and enrollments shrinking; on the other, a small but fervently committed group of students and their families found an affordable, publicly supported educational alternative that met their needs better than the traditional school model. The controversy was largely resolved when the state legislature agreed to rewrite the charter law and pick up 30 percent of the cost to the home districts for all charter school students, regardless of whether they transfer to cyber charters or the brick-and-mortar kind. The changes to Pennsylvania's charter school law prompted by the Western controversy particularly benefited large districts such as Philadelphia's, which owed charters more per-student spending money and who had more students going to charter schools.

Despite the political trial by fire, the cyber charter has been a boon to the regional economy and has helped reframe the statewide debate about public education, according to Nick Trombetta, the Midland district superintendent and the chief administrative officer of Western. The cyber charter, which expects an enrollment of 1,700 for the 2003–2004 school year, has become "an economic engine," he says. He estimates that it brings $7 to $9 million into the local economy, providing new jobs and demand for local services. (It also pays 75 percent of Trombetta's salary.) This entrepreneurial aspect of cyber schooling has also changed the ways in which Midland's educators think about the relationship between students and school districts. "We've learned to speak as businesspeople because this has turned into a huge undertaking. We talk about 'markets,' and we talk about what the market requires and how to meet the needs of the customers. The students are clients and we treat them as such," Trombetta says. He acknowledges, though, that cyber charters may not be the most efficient models, duplicating services and costing the state too much. Rather, he argues in favor of a system where cyber schools supplement existing district programs rather than replace them.

Pennsylvania is not alone in debating the merits of the cyber charter model. Across the nation, critics have questioned the high number of homeschooled students benefiting from cyber charter funding—as many as 56 percent were previously homeschooled—raising concerns about whether it is fair to let homeschoolers opt out of regular schools and still tap into a resource that requires a disproportionately high amount of district funding. Some state charter laws anticipated such questions of equity, with Colorado's charter law specifically banning online schools from enrolling students who were previously taught at home or went to private school.

On the flip side, Idaho's state-operated online school has faced opposition from homeschool families, who see it as a way for the state government to infiltrate homeschool culture (Snell, 2002). The tensions around cyber chartering are not trivial, particularly since this model overtly shifts money between different types of schools. It could take several years before the most workable model for cyber charter schools takes shape. Cyber charters may represent a transitional approach that will familiarize the larger K–12 public with an innovative modality for learning for a time, until it is ultimately incorporated as a permanent option in all public school systems.

The Challenge of Startup Costs

Even when cyber schools are meant to supplement rather than replace regular schools, the political and economic challenges are formidable. By early 2003, at least 16 states already had constructed online learning programs that focused on supplementing existing traditional education, rather than offering competitive, alternative programs like that of Pennsylvania's Midland district.

Florida has pioneered the most sweeping model of online supplemental education. The Florida Virtual School (FLVS) offers a full range of courses free of charge to in-state students and stops just short of offering a diploma. Other states, including Kentucky, Michigan, New Mexico, Alabama, and, most recently, Maryland, have followed the spirit of this model. In most cases, financing came from states alone or from a combination of state funding and tuition.

Sponsors have typically framed their mission as offering equity of educational opportunity and quality to public school students in an era when teacher shortages, budget cuts, and other realities of public schooling have caused uneven course quality in public schools. In this model, students usually have the option of taking the courses from home- or school-based computer labs. Students enroll through contractual agreements between their districts and the state online school.

Although this approach deflects the political heat surrounding the cyber charter model, it does incur high startup costs for creating courses and purchasing web-based course platform technology. In Florida's case, in the first two years of the program, the state poured $6.1 million into the startup by a team of teachers and designers from Orange and Alachua county school districts, and there was additional funding and in-kind support from business partners. Michigan is estimated to have spent $12 million on its online schooling program. The University of Nebraska designed its statewide course offerings through a five-year, $15 million federal grant, and then established a separate commercial entity, Class.com, which administers the program.

The growth of these programs among a small but devoted segment of the public is evident. For example, since its founding in 1997, FLVS's enrollment has grown from a mere 77 Florida students to 11,000 students in the 2002–2003 school year, the largest enrollment among the K–12 programs. These students come from both inside Florida and out of state, with the outsiders paying tuition. In the 2003–2004 school year, 75 courses will be offered and taught by 100 teachers. The program has expanded to include middle school courses and GED programs. Florida's program boasts an 80 percent course completion rate and a 70 percent qualifying rate for students who take its Advanced Placement courses. As in Pennsylvania, the Florida programs also appear to be satisfying the original stated needs for choice and quality, as evidenced by a parent survey that showed 93 percent of a sample of 663 parents reported they would recommend the program to other parents. The Florida program would not appear to be meeting goals for equity, however, as 79 percent of the students were white and only 21 percent were minority in the 2000–2001 school year, in a state where 48.6 percent of the students were minority students that year. One trend noted by FLVS leaders was that students opted to take some courses on line, such as government, so that they could sign up for other more preferable courses at their schools. "Surprisingly enough, the most popular courses are the ones students can get at their local school," said Bruce Friend, FLVS's chief academic officer. "It's freeing up space to take something else at their local school."

Not every state is going to have the kind of growth that an early pioneer such as Florida has had. Newcomers must consider the costs of establishing and maintaining quality online programs. One vice president of Apex Learning, an online learning program focused on Advanced Placement courses, has estimated that it takes $100,000 to $200,000, 15 people, and nearly eight months to develop a single online course lasting a semester or year (NASBE, 2001). These costs have led many more recent entrants to the statewide online learning arena to offer a mix of courses that are locally developed and pre-made by commercial vendors, such as Class.com and Apex.

The newer online learning providers also tend to use existing delivery platforms offered by vendors such as Blackboard and eCollege. Purchasing such services is costly. KMPG Consulting found in their analysis of Pennsylvania's cyber charter schools that the per-student costs ranged from around $5,000 to $7,000, roughly equivalent to the per-student costs at brick-and-mortar schools. KMPG concluded that, while cyber charter schools may be a less costly form of education than the brick-and-mortar type, "not all new cyber schools have long-term viability" (KMPG, 2001, p. 5). They described the advantages of cyber schools as being able to leverage school staff while students rely more on parents and having fewer costs associated with building maintenance, transportation, and food service.

On the other hand, cyber schools spend a greater portion of their budgets on technology, curriculum development, and support staff to improve the interaction with students than regular schools. Smaller cyber schools with fewer than 200 students would face challenges trying to spread such costs, but those with more than 500 students would function better. Other agencies have also raised questions about the financial viability of some cyber charter schools. The federal Web-Based Education Commission led by former Nebraska senator Bob Kerrey found that, unless "school districts and states create significant demand for innovative online learning materials, it may not be economically feasible for many online education content providers to stay in business." This would lead to a domination of the market by a few providers, limited choice, and possible stagnation of innovation and design.

Despite the financial investment required, sponsors of these statewide supplemental education ventures believe such services can help U.S. public schools provide more flexible access to education. Some even see the online medium as potentially having a positive impact on pedagogy in traditional education. "I think it is going to be a significant driver for reform," said Steven Sanchez, acting assistant superintendent for learning at the New Mexico Department of Education. "We've already seen that here in New Mexico, where people are really questioning, 'Well, you know, how *do* we support kids?' It has really started getting people to examine their beliefs about kids. I think teachers will look at their face-to-face kids in a new way."

In Sanchez's view, students in an online environment have less tolerance for courses in which a teacher controls the interaction, as in a typical lecture-style classroom. Ultimately, New Mexico has learned, as did VHS, that the medium requires the instructor to try other approaches to engage learners more interactively in activities and discussion. Sanchez observed that there was still much to be learned about enhancing interactivity in online courses. He mentioned that "virtual field trips" represented a first step, but he wanted to see more exploration of interactivity, such as a virtual science lab or online science tools that students could use to collect data in their local communities.

The work of K–12 online learning pioneers suggests that the new medium is attaining a degree of stability as a viable avenue for K–12 student learning, especially for the small but vocal groups of students and their families who seek supplements and alternatives to traditional schooling. Online learning has also infused some sorely needed customer service principles into the staid realm of public education.

It may be several years before the K–12 public reaches consensus on how much online learning will supplement or compete with existing public education. In some ways, public educators find the online option an improvement on its services. In others, public educators question the waste and duplication involved in financing some modes of providing online education. Of course, there remain many questions about the ultimate viability of the system. It could take a generation or two before a larger segment of the K–12 public perceives online learning as a natural alternative to the brick-and-mortar school.

Beyond such political and financial considerations, though, online learning will ultimately be judged by what impact it has on student achievement, especially in the standards-based, high-stakes-testing world. More than one online pioneer has told of a student who had failed in traditional settings but succeeded online. These stories are still too scattered and few to constitute data for a scientific study, but they speak to the timeless and core value in American education: providing educational opportunity for all. As Nick Trombetta of the Western Pennsylvania Cyber Charter School says, "We've learned that it's not about the technology. It's about the people."

References

Clark, T. (2001). *Virtual schools: Trends and issues.* Macomb: Western Illinois University, The Center for the Application of Information Technologies.

Collison, G., Elbaum, B., Haavind, S., & Tinker, R. (2000). *Facilitating online learning: Effective strategies for moderators.* Madison, WI: Atwood.

Florida Department of Education. (2002). *Long term growth of minority student population in Florida's public schools.* Retrieved June 6, 2003, from http://www.firn.edu/doe/eias/eiaspubs/pdf/minority.pdf

Institute for Higher Education Policy (IHEP). (2000). *Quality on the line.* Washington, DC: Author. Retrieved May 7, 2003, from http://www.ihep.com/Pubs/PDF/Quality.pdf

KPMG Consulting. (2001). *Cyber charter schools review.* Harrisburg: Pennsylvania Department of Education.

National Association of State Boards of Education (NASBE). (2001). *Any time, any place, any path, any pace: Taking the lead on e-learning policy.* Alexandria, VA: Author.

National Center for Education Statistics (NCES). (1997–1998). *Distance education at postsecondary education institutions: 1997–1998.* Washington, DC: Author. Retrieved May 13, 2003, from http://nces.ed.gov/pubsearch/pubsinfo.asp?pubid=2000013

NCES. (1999). *Homeschooling in the United States: 1999*. Washington, DC: Author. Retrieved May 13, 2003, from http://nces.ed.gov/pubsearch/pubsinfo. asp?pubid=2001033

NCES. (1999–2000). *Public charter school survey*. Washington, DC: Author. Retrieved May 13, 2003, from http://nces.ed.gov/programs/coe/2002/pdf/ 30_2002.pdf

NCES. (2001). *Common core of data*. Washington, DC: Author. Retrieved May 13, 2003, from http://nces.ed.gov/ccd/bat/Result.asp?id=468350669& CurPage=2&view=State

Optimal Performance. (2001). *The Florida Virtual School parent survey*. Washington, DC: Author. Retrieved June 6, 2003, from http://www.flvs.net/ _about_us/pdf_au/flvs_parent_survey_results.pdf

Snell, L. (2002). *Cyber schools compete with traditional public schools*. Los Angeles: Reason Public Policy Institute. Retrieved May 13, 2003, from http:// www.rppi.org/cyberschools.html

How Handhelds Can Have an Impact in the Classroom: The Teacher Perspective

By Cathleen A. Norris and Elliot Soloway

Technology has long held out promises for having a significant impact on K–12 education. Each new wave of innovation—mainframes, timesharing, desktops, the Internet—rekindles those expectations. Sadly, K–12 schools are still standing at the altar, waiting for the long-promised results. Indeed, while the Internet has brought about positive changes in many areas of everyday life, including commerce and government, K–12 schools have gotten precious little of value from it.

The arrival of another generation of technology—handheld computers—also raises skeptical questions about the potential impact of these powerful new tools: Given our poor track record, why should anyone believe the technology enthusiasts? What is so different about handheld computers?

We believe the promise of handheld computers will in fact be realized because, in contrast to desktop/laptop technologies, handhelds more effectively address the major concerns of teachers. These concerns, as we have identified them in our research, include:

1. **Student outcomes:** How do handheld computers support productive learning activities and how do they enable teachers to assess learning progress?
2. **Curriculum:** Handhelds do afford students and teachers the opportunity to carry out important learning activities.
3. **Classroom management:** Managing devices, students, and artifacts when 30 children use handhelds for all classroom activities can definitely be a challenge.
4. **Learning environment:** Handhelds disappear into existing learning spaces, unlike their bigger desktop/laptop relations.

For the past 25 years or so, we have been working to understand how to extract the value of technology for K–12 education. The data (Honey, 2001; Norris, Smolka, & Soloway, 2000) suggest that, when the conditions are right, technology can indeed have a demonstrable, positive impact on teaching and learning. (The conditions for success include sufficient access to technology, relevant curriculum, adequate professional development, appropriate assessments, supportive administration, and supportive parents and community. No real surprises here—these are needed for any educational innovation to work.) Still, though U.S. schools have spent billions of dollars on computing technologies, there still is a fundamental problem with access. First, the ratio of students to computers is 5.4 to 1 in general, and 9 to 1 in urban settings (U.S. Department of Commerce, 2000), which is far lower than is necessary for technology to have a significant impact. Second, of the teachers we have surveyed, 60 percent say that they have a single computer or none at all in their classrooms.

Technology can't have an impact if children aren't using the technology. Thus, although technology naysayers (Cordes & Miller, 1999; Healy, 1998; Stoll, 1995) typically try to point to something inherently bad about technology as the reason technology hasn't had an impact in K–12, the plain and simple fact is that K–12 students, except in isolated pockets, haven't had sufficient access to technology to really give it an opportunity to make a difference.

However, with the emergence of low-cost handheld computers, 1:1 access is finally conceivable. Indeed, on July 18, 2003, the Michigan legislature, following the precedent set in Maine, passed a bill appropriating $40 million to provide each and every sixth grader in Michigan—or about 132,000 students—his/her own personal, wireless computer. For the $300 per student the legislature is making available, laptops are not a viable option, but a plethora of handheld computers can fit the bill.

In fact, over the next three years, most U.S. states will pass similar measures. By the end of this first decade of the new millennium, every U.S. public school student will, without question, have his/her own handheld computer that is accessible in class and at home, on the school bus and at the soccer field, outside at the river while collecting water quality data, and on Saturday morning during a gym workout. The turning point is upon us; it is no longer a question of if children will be getting handheld computers, but when and how.

Since 1999, we have been working in a range of classrooms around the country exploring the strengths and weaknesses of handheld computers for K–12. For example, we have worked in third-grade classrooms in Michigan and Texas and middle school classrooms in these and other states. In our experience, high schools have been slower in their adoption of handheld technologies, but we are now seeing them start pilot projects. The observations presented here are based on our experiences working with more than a thousand students in several states.

With that preamble, we are now ready to dive into a description of how the use of handheld computers can address the major concerns of K–12 teachers.

Improving Student Learning

The core concerns for a teacher are 1) making sure that students engage in productive learning activities and 2) making sure that there is a way to assess a student's progress. In classrooms where each child has a handheld computer, both of these issues can be addressed in a natural, non-onerous way. Paper-based classrooms and desktop/laptop-based classrooms do not address these issues as directly and easily.

First, handhelds make a range of productive learning activities easier or more interesting for students. For example:

- **Writing and rewriting:** In numerous classrooms, we have seen how using handhelds encourages children to write and then revise their writing, based on teacher and peer comments. Why do children readily write and rewrite using handhelds? No magic here: It's all about access—again. Since the handhelds are literally at one's fingertips, access to students' writings is a tap away. In contrast, if a child writes on one of the very few classroom computers—or worse, writes on one in the computer lab—that child needs to go back to the original computer (or a computer on the network, if a network is available) to revise. But, since access to computers is problematic and scheduling of activities in schools is also fraught with change, getting back to that original document is seldom easy. (We hasten to point out that keyboards must be provided to support writing. It has been our experience that children will use a stylus to write a short paragraph, but they will not write longer documents unless they are using a keyboard.)

- **Collaborating:** Artifacts are the bridges that sustain extended collaboration, but exchanging paper-based artifacts is problematic and limits the types of collaboration that can take place. Similarly, if documents are on a computer that is not readily accessible to all members of a team, collaboration is hampered. However, with handhelds, team members can "beam" documents in seconds from one handheld to another. In the FreeWrite text editor developed by the Center for Highly Interactive Computing in Education (HI-CE) at the University of Michigan, we have built in an *exchange beam,* which enables a pair of students to swap documents in one action. Similarly, peer editing becomes logistically easy to do: beam, review, and beam back.

- **Reviewing:** Studying for a test means reviewing your notes— if you can find your notes. "Mom, have you seen . . . ?" is a typical student question. But again, if the notes are on the handheld computer that goes everywhere with the student, finding those notes is no longer a problem.

Second, by creating a digital portfolio that captures a child's work, handhelds can improve assessment. That is, in a typical classroom a child will have some work done on paper and some work done on a computer. As such, there is no central, cumulative repository for that work. In such a situation, it is hard to really grasp how much change occurs over a semester, how much learning takes place and is reflected in a child's work over the school year. In contrast, if all the work a child does—from note taking to group projects—is done on the child's handheld, then there is a permanent record that can be periodically inspected and reviewed. (Clearly, work produced on a handheld computer must be backed up since invariably there will be crashes and lost files. We return to this issue later.)

Improving the Curriculum

In order to facilitate the adoption of handheld computers in K–12, we point out two mistakes technology enthusiasts made in the past—with an eye toward not making them again.

1. **"Teachers, handheld computers have a great number of super features."** Yes, but . . . schools don't want technology, schools want curriculum. We repeat that point, which technology enthusiasts often miss: Schools don't want technology, schools want curriculum. Just as mainframe computers with time-sharing, and more recently the Internet, are not the point, handheld computers per se also are not. Teachers and students are not evaluated based on the number of computers they have or their speed of access to the Internet, but rather on the learning that takes place using those computers' access to the Internet. It is curricular needs that should drive the use of technology.

2. **"Teachers, in order to use the computer (or any new technology), you will need to change your instructional practices completely."** In the early days of computing, some version of that sentence was used to introduce and close professional develop-

ment workshops. For example, we asked teachers to teach computer programming, thinking that learning to program was the way to add value to learning from technology. We asked teachers to write computer programs for their students since there was little educational software available. We asked teachers to give up control of their class and let an ILS—Integrated Learning System—manage and deliver instruction to the students. We asked them to adopt "constructivist learning" and allow students to discover math and science principles. While teachers were too polite to say "I don't think so," they did vote with their feet. Precious few did change—and why should they have? Why should they dispense with strategies and intuitions gained from 20 to 30 years of classroom practice to use a totally unproven instructional innovation?

Today, in introducing handhelds in a professional development workshop we (the authors) start out by saying, "Evolution, not revolution." In *Crossing the Chasm*, the Silicon Valley bible of technology diffusion, Geoffrey Moore (1991) uses this expression to reflect the strategy for reaching the conservative, risk-averse individuals who make up the "early majority." We take a similar approach with teachers. To start out using handhelds, we suggest that teachers use their existing curriculum and existing instructional strategies—with just a *little* change.

For example, if teachers use concept mapping as a learning activity, we suggest that they do that activity using PicoMap, a concept mapping application, on a PalmOS or PocketPC-based handheld. Now, in using PicoMap, the teachers can have the children collaborate (e.g., two students work together on a concept map) or peer edit (e.g., one student critiques the concept map of another student) by using the infrared beaming function. With one tap of the stylus, a student can send a concept map to another student's handheld in seconds.

Success breeds confidence. Based on the success of this activity, teachers are more likely to be willing to change their instructional practices a bit more in order to benefit even more from the technology. For example, using the full suite of office productivity tools for the PalmOS developed by our research group, HI-CE, and distributed by GoKnow, Inc. (www.goknow.com),* teachers can work up to having their children use their handheld computers 100 percent of the time in school—as opposed to the 10 percent of the time that desktop or laptops are used. In effect, a handheld computer is simply a "supersized" notebook. It is something that can be used by students on a routine, day-in, day-out basis, with little fanfare or hoopla. But a handheld-based notebook affords opportunities for learning that can't be provided by its paper-based cousin.

Currently, there is a dearth of content materials available for handhelds. We hear this lament primarily from high school teachers. For example, textbooks are still printed on paper, the vast majority of computer-based educational applications are still available only for personal computers, and educationally relevant websites are, for the most part, not effectively viewable on the small screen of a handheld. Frankly, this situation is a short-term one; as handhelds become more widely adopted, the economics will encourage content developers to make their materials available for handhelds.

---

* At http://www.goknow.com, one can download free a word processor, a spreadsheet, a drawing/animation program, an offline web browsing tool, and several other educational applications for the PalmOS handhelds. At http://hi-ce.org/pocketpc, a comparable set of applications for the PocketPC platform can be downloaded.

Better Classroom Management

Limited access to technology (e.g., one or two computers in a class-room, a computer lab down the hall) certainly increases the burden on the teacher to manage a scarce resource effectively. But does 100 percent access to handhelds also place too big a burden on teachers? The potential is surely there. Although the barriers to initial use of handhelds are low, scaling up to 100 percent use must be done with careful planning.

Broadly speaking, there are two strategies for managing handheld devices in the classroom, the rotational model and the personal model. We prefer the personal model.

- **Rotational model:** Each child is given a handheld computer for a specific task during the school day, such as a concept-mapping activity. The handheld is collected after the activity. We find the rotational model employed when funding is low and only one set of handhelds can be purchased, and where it is felt that all children should have a turn at using a handheld. In this situation, the burden for managing the devices does fall on the teacher. He/she must ensure that the batteries are charged up, that the programs to be used are included on the handheld, and that programs that shouldn't be loaded (e.g., games) are not included. Frankly, this is an onerous burden—charging 30 handhelds or swapping batteries on 30 student devices is a very time-consuming activity. In our experience, we have found that classes that employ the rotational model end up not using the handhelds very much. Although the intent is to provide everyone with access, the upshot is that no one has access since keeping the units running falls on the back of the teacher—who already has enough to do!

- **Personal model**: Each child in a class is issued a handheld at the beginning of the school year for the entire year. The student might well be able to take it home after an initial, in-school-only period. Will students steal the units or sell them for drugs? Will students drop the units or mistreat them? In four years, these potential concerns have remained just that—potential concerns. With the personal model, we have found that the children take ownership and responsibility for the maintenance of the unit.

Another issue that teachers must deal with when students use handhelds is how to manage students who are using portable technology in collaborative ways. For example, once students start beaming documents to each other, there is no way to enforce a no talking/no walking policy. The energy and excitement surrounding beaming is infectious—and it can be pedagogically productive. But, for these sorts of collaborative interactions to take place, a teacher must feel comfortable with a classroom that can be a bit noisy and in flux.

We have found that, over the course of one school year, each student will generate upwards of 100 documents on his/her handheld computer, not counting revisions and intermediate documents. And, what happens when one of the boys in the class puts the 29th game on his handheld and locks it up so that a hard reset is needed and all the documents are lost? How does a teacher retrieve assignment #4 from each of the handhelds, grade them, and provide individualized feedback? How does a teacher distribute a book report form to each student?

Frankly, infrared beaming will not reach this level of communication; beaming works for quick, one-shot sharing, but not for class-level, secure movement of documents. And, while children might have no trouble reading documents on a handheld screen, bifocal-

Figure 1   The Synching Solution for Palm® OS Handhelds in Education

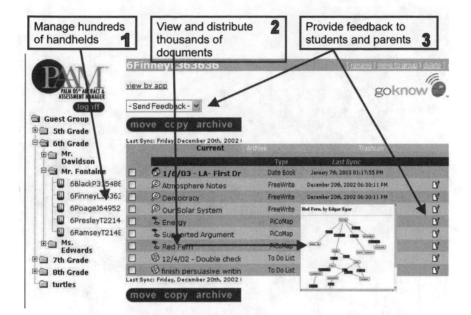

generation teachers need some digital assistance for reading multi-page documents.

Again, inasmuch as it is early in the deployment of handhelds in classrooms, there are few document management systems available. Figure 1 presents a screen image from GoKnow's Pocket Artifact and Assessment Manager (PAAM) that runs in a web browser. Students put their handhelds into a cradle attached to a desktop computer and then PAAM retrieves all the student-generated documents from the handheld and sends them to a server, over the Internet. The students' teacher (or parents or principal) can then view the documents in a web browser; the teacher can send comments about the document back to the student

Figure 2   Third Graders Using Handhelds in a Beanbag Chair

using PAAM. In time, there will be more systems like PAAM from which a school can choose. However, based on our experience, it is clear that a teacher needs a PAAM-like system if he or she adopts the personal model.

Better Learning Environments

Before handhelds, computers were not particularly friendly devices for teachers trying to create appealing learning spaces. Recall the advertisements for "Integrated Learning Systems" that depicted 30 children in a computer lab, each child with eyes glued to the computer screen and

Figure 3 Seventh Graders Using Handhelds in the School Library

tethered to a computer by headphones and thus isolated from each other and from the teacher.

Now contrast that with the photograph of third graders using handhelds while sitting in a beanbag chair (Figure 2) and seventh graders using handheld computers in the school library (Figure 3). Clearly, handheld computers, unlike their desktop and laptop relations, can be easily integrated into the physical fabric where learning takes place.

HI-CE has been working in 28 middle schools in Detroit for the past five years, attempting to bring an inquiry-driven, standards-based, technology-enhanced curriculum to science classrooms. After this period of working closely with the science teachers in these schools, approximately 50 percent of them now use the Artemis Digital Library, a learner-centered research engine we developed, during the implementation of the science units. In contrast, 87 percent of the science teachers used the Cooties activity, a handheld-based program that helps children understand how diseases are spread, during its first year of availability.

Teachers clearly see handhelds as easy to use and low maintenance; furthermore, handhelds are not particularly intimidating. They can fit into existing instructional practices, but those practices will change over time as teachers grow more comfortable and more expert in using handhelds with their students. As this happens, K–12 schools will finally reap the benefits long promised by modern computing technologies.

References

Cordes, C., & Miller, E. (1999). *Fool's gold: A critical look at computers in childhood*. College Park, MD: Alliance for Childhood. Available online at http://www.allianceforchildhood.net/

Healy, J. (1998). *Failure to connect: How computers affect our children's minds and what we can do about it*. New York: Simon & Schuster.

Honey, M. (2001). Testimony before the Labor, HHS, and Education appropriations subcommittee, United States Senate, July 25, 2001. Available online at http://main.edc.org/newsroom/features/mhtestimony.asp

Moore, G.A. (1991). *Crossing the chasm: Marketing and selling high-tech goods to mainstream customers*. New York: Harper Business.

Norris, C., Smolka, J., & Soloway, E. (2000). Extracting value from research: A guide for the perplexed. *Technology and Learning, 20*(11), 45–48.

Stoll, C. (1995). *Silicon snake oil: Second thoughts on the information highway*. New York: Doubleday.

U.S. Department of Commerce. (2000). *Statistical abstract of the United States.* Washington, DC: Author. Available online at http://www.census.gov/prod/www/statistical-abstract-us.html

Acknowledgments

The work described here is supported in part by Intel and the National Science Foundation (NSF) under grant number NSF ITR 0085946. Any opinions, findings, and conclusions or recommendations expressed in this material are those of the authors and do not necessarily reflect those of the NSF.

Linking Teachers with Technology for Professional Development and Support

By David T. Gordon

T he task of providing education professionals with high-quality staff development has taken on fresh urgency since the passage of the federal No Child Left Behind (NCLB) Act, which essentially mandates improvements in the quality of the nation's teaching corps by 2006. While much of what passes for in-service training often consists of one-day sessions with little connection to actual classroom goals, research shows that successful professional development will be focused sharply on classroom instruction and content. It will be collaborative, intensive, and sustained, giving participants opportunities to examine and critique their own practice and one another's. Strategies may include having master teachers mentor novices, organizing collaborative discussions of student work around curricular goals, and using lesson-study groups to share best practices and evaluate classroom instruction.

No longer marooned behind the closed doors of their classrooms, teachers with high-quality professional development and support (especially novices) are more likely to stay on the job, according to research conducted by the Harvard Project on the Next Generation of Teachers. And studies by the Consortium on Chicago School Research show that high-quality professional development can lead to improvements in students' classroom achievement as well.

Writing in the journal *Educational Researcher*, James Hiebert, Ronald Gallimore, and James W. Stigler discuss the need for "a knowledge base [for the teaching profession] that grows and improves." Such a resource, they write, must begin with "practitioner knowledge—the kinds of knowledge practitioners generate through active participation and reflection on their own practice." But it would also be enhanced by contributions from educational research, provided that research is translated into forms teachers can use to improve their classroom practice. The authors admit that building this knowledge base—that is, turning practitioner knowledge into professional knowledge—while bridging the gap between research and practice is no small challenge. Professional knowledge, they argue, must be communicable.

Just as important, it must be communicated. And that's where new technologies may make a difference. Thanks to improvements in desktop systems, Internet connections, digital audio and video, web conferencing, and more, the potential for creating a wide-scale professional knowledge base for teachers has never been greater. Thanks to these technologies, efforts to collect, sort, store, and share examples of best classroom practices are far easier now than they would have been just a few years ago. For example, video case studies of lessons offered through web-based digital libraries are one potentially powerful resource for teachers, Hiebert et al. point out. Using such libraries in combination with online conferencing and courses could make significant contributions to the development of the professional knowledge base the authors describe.

In 2003, the National Commission on Teaching and America's Future, a Washington, D.C.-based nonprofit group of educators, policymakers, and business leaders, issued a major report that made a strong case for professional development to sharpen the expertise of teachers through collegial study and coaching. The report, entitled *No Dream Denied: A Pledge to America's Children*, identified new technologies as a potentially powerful aid for delivering the kind of professional support system teachers need to transform their classroom practice:

> Technology provides the means to create and support teachers in learning communities. These communities can be based entirely within a school, providing teachers with a "place" in which to meet within the busy school day—or they can extend across schools, districts, states, or even nations to provide much broader communities of practice.

Of course, finding the means to develop such meaningful communities of practice is not enough. Indeed, the greatest barriers may not be logistical or even technological but cultural. The teaching profession is hampered by long-standing structures that have each teacher deciding what and how to teach in "their" classrooms—what Harvard researcher Richard F. Elmore calls the "cult of connoisseurship." This can impede efforts to scale up reforms even at the school level, not to mention the profession as a whole.

But for those who really do want the sustained, intensive professional development and support that research shows they need, the logistical obstacles can be significant. It takes enormous commitments of resources and time to bring people together in frequent, face-to-face settings. Schools have to organize release time, arrange substitute teachers, and find the funds. Teachers have to coordinate their schedules, organize child care, use the family car, and spend time traveling from home to the setting. There are likely to be fewer choices in traditional course offerings than in online settings. And once a traditional, face-to-face session has finished, there is often little opportunity for follow-up discussion and collaboration.

Whether through formal online courses or informal web-based networks, educators now have opportunities to develop communities of practice and get in-service instruction in ways that are flexible, convenient, and sustained—opportunities that their predecessors never had.

What do such innovations look like in practice? One example of online professional development is the program WIDE World (Wide-scale Interactive Development for Educators at http://www.wideworld. pz.harvard.edu), developed at the Harvard Graduate School of Education to offer training in assessment, curriculum development, integration of new technologies, and the use of educational models such as "Teaching for Understanding" (TfU). Blending the advantages of personal instruction with the flexibility of working on line, participants log on for text-based "lectures" and supplementary materials, take part in group activities, and post their work. They form small learning groups of ten, which are led by a coach and organized around participants' interests or goals, levels of expertise, and subject areas. Students get step-by-step feedback from instructors, coaches, and fellow participants, and they benefit from the perspectives of fellow professionals from all over the world. Since WIDE formed in 1999, attendees have included teachers and administrators from dozens of countries, including Namibia, Pakistan, and Colombia.

"If the goal is to help practitioners perform better in the real world, then there are remarkable advantages that networked communication technologies offer over traditional professional development," says Martha Stone Wiske, director of Harvard's Education with New Technologies website (http://learnweb.harvard.edu/ent) and one of the organizers of WIDE World. She notes that traditional staff development tends to be delivered in one-shot sessions, which provide no opportunity for teachers to think over what they have learned and follow up with other participants. Also, topics often are chosen by a district and don't quite match teachers' concerns or interests, which goes against what research says is effective in adult education. "Adults want to learn about things that they feel are important. They want some choice, given their competing priorities, over what they learn," says Wiske. "They want to share their expertise with others, and they want to connect that learning to their work."

Getting practitioners to try out new ideas, solicit feedback from peers and mentors, reflect on their work, and make plans to revise their practice—this all may be easier to accomplish in an online setting that doesn't require everyone to be together at the same place and time. Unlike a traditional class, where comments and sharing are limited by time, the online course may actually offer more interaction among learners, says Wiske. With a good facilitator the format encourages everyone to exchange comments, debate ideas, share drafts, and discuss classroom experiments. The result, she says, is that "all the expertise of participants and all their emerging insights become a source of energy and a resource for learning that, in face-to-face formats, is usually hidden."

Challenges and Expectations

Similar advantages are demonstrated in a study of a web-based course for in-service teachers by Fordham University researcher Kathleen P. King. The federally sponsored program combined traditional, face-to-face seminars (6 sessions) with web-based, interactive classes (8 sessions)—a so-called hybrid model. Email, file-sharing, and video-conferencing technologies were used for reflection and discussion among the students, all of whom were educational professionals of diverse backgrounds, experience, and technical knowledge. (Participants also got a phone number and email address for technical assistance.) King notes that the online format was tailored to fit with what research shows are the principles of successful adult learning: 1) to build on prior knowledge, 2) to encourage active, respectful participation and collaborative inquiry, and 3) to focus on practical, action-based lessons.

Interestingly, prior to the course, participants did not have high expectations for its online portion. Many expected a highly impersonal experience with little interaction among participants. However, King's survey shows that the online learning was not the solitary endeavor participants expected. In fact, many reported that they actually had more productive exchanges with classmates than they usually did in a face-to-face class. They were especially surprised—and professionally nourished—by the extent and depth of responses from other participants to their postings to online discussion forums. The more these students used online tools, the more comfortable and savvy they were at using the format—a sign that the participants were developing a community of practice over time. Of course, this didn't happen in a vacuum. King's study shows that successful online learning required a good facilitator who carefully chose the topics and provided adequate guidance, especially in the beginning. The online facilitator had to communicate clear expectations and instructions and find ways of making up for the subtle cues and communication that a traditional instructor might use in a face-to-face format.

For online learning to succeed, participants have to adjust their expectations of what their roles and activities in the class will entail, according to a study of Indiana University's Collaborative Teacher Education Program (CTEP). Published by *T.H.E. Journal* [Technological Horizons in Education] in 2000, the study focused on K–12 teachers and administrators who were taking CTEP's online professional development course for the first time. Participants, most of whom represented rural districts, did field-based activities in their schools, then exchanged documents, traded feedback, and got instruction using web-based conferencing tools.

The experience often produced significant anxiety and discomfort among those who were used to traditional instruction. Potential roadblocks identified by the authors included the absence of a live instructor, the strangeness of the format, and the new set of tasks that participants were expected to perform. This, added to the prospect of technical snafus, may have made participants wary of online learning.

But the greatest challenge to course participants was to adjust their own expectations of what it means to teach and learn, according to the researchers. The online-learning experience demanded more self-direction and collaborative effort than the teacher-centered model that participants themselves practiced in schools. For that reason, CTEP instructors assumed that a student-directed learning approach was unfamiliar to most teachers—that they had to be showed how to develop independence and take an active role in their own learning.

The classes started with a gradual introduction to technology use and a traditional, "instructor-centered" approach. Instructors led carefully scripted discussions and gave students plenty of time to develop their written answers. At this stage, communication was generally limited to two-way emails between instructors and learners. After a few weeks, instructors loosened the format and encouraged participants to share in-school experiences and teaching methods with each other, to take part in "getting-to-know-you" exercises to foster confidence and collegiality, and to perform lighthearted surveys.

Once the lines of communication were opened among learners, they began using more sophisticated web tools for discussions and document sharing. Working in groups of various sizes, they discussed course concepts, shared work experiences, and offered one another suggestions for carrying out assignments and improving teaching practices. The public nature of these postings encouraged learners to take greater care in developing their responses and to learn from the helpful models of their peers. The class then broke into small teams for web-based assignments, where the interaction among participants intensified. The result of the study was plain, according to the researchers. For distance learning to work, both instructors and learners had to make an extra effort to adopt a different model for teaching and learning, one that was collaborative and required students to take control of their own educational experience.

Online Communities

In addition to formal Internet courses like CTEP, teachers are finding many new opportunities for informal professional collaboration and exchange through networked technologies. Those faced with isolation and poor development options in their districts can now join one of a growing number of online discussion groups or web communities. One the best known—indeed, pioneering—examples is Tapped In (http://www.tappedin.org), a project begun in 1995 at the research organization SRI International, with support from the National Science Foundation and Sun Microsystems.

Tapped In's founders set out to develop "an online education community of practice" where education professionals could network. Each month, some 12,000 teachers and administrators log in to discuss curriculum and practice, take "e-courses" and workshops, plan and conduct projects with colleagues and students, and trade information about every conceivable aspect of schooling.

Teachers may set up their own "personal offices," where they can post electronic portfolios and lesson plans, helpful articles and resources, and even personal photos, anecdotes, favorite quotations, and other items. Organizers also hope to develop a formal library system of web links, articles, and other materials that are posted in these offices or used in e-courses—resources that would be rated by users much the way books are on Amazon.com and other online sites. "Teachers like this idea a lot because they usually don't get an office at work," says Judi Fusco, Tapped In's director of community activities. "It's much more than a flashy gizmo. It gives them a place to organize their ideas and share their practice with others."

In the Afterschool Online program, twenty or so volunteer teachers staff an online reception area every afternoon, greeting teachers as they log on, answering questions, and offering advice for finding resources. A regular calendar of web events is also available. For example, one discussion group is titled "Moving Every Child Ahead: An Alternative Approach to the Goals of No Child Left Behind." The discussion question: "Can we build a community of 'studied interventions' where groups of educators share the evidence they generate through their daily actions with kids?" Another, more lighthearted option is to ask "The Frugal Educator" where to get good classroom materials on the cheap.

At the end of a visit, Tapped In users receive an email with a complete transcript of their online interactions—a take-away, printable record of the advice they gave and received to consult at a later time. Just be careful what you call those online meeting areas: They're not chat rooms. As Fusco says, "Nobody wants to *chat*. We don't use that word." The message is clear: Professionals confer, meet, and discuss; nonprofessionals chat.

In addition to these more casual offerings, Tapped In also provides a portal to formal online courses. For example, Pepperdine University is a "tenant" in the Tapped In "building," offering online courses from its teacher-education program. The benefits have been mutual, says Tapped In founder and director Mark Schlager. In addition to drawing students Pepperdine's way, Tapped In benefits from Pepperdine graduates who continue to use the resource even as they have fanned out into school systems throughout the United States. Other tenants include the Milwaukee public school system, which uses Tapped In for teacher discussions and support.

What's Next?

As technology advances, Tapped In and other nonprofits of its kind are faced with a number of challenges. One is that while evolving technologies will offer new opportunities to facilitate teacher-to-teacher interaction, there is always a danger that service providers will get out ahead of teachers and their technology capabilities, says Schlager. For instance, live videoconferencing is not yet a practical solution because it requires, among other things, cameras on computers and huge amounts of bandwidth.

But digital video libraries, which don't require the computing power of live video, can already serve as powerful tools for professional learning. For example, visit the California Learning Interchange (http://www.gse.uci.edu/cli), a service created by the University of California–Irvine, Apple Computer, and the Orange County public schools. In addition to providing teachers with a variety of tips and web links, the site offers video of master teachers demonstrating expert classroom instruction, organized by subject area (e.g., history, science, English/language arts), as well as instructional videos about cognitive development, learning theories, multicultural education, and more.

The George Lucas Educational Foundation (http://www.glef.org) also offers best-practices video, as does the North Central Regional Technology in Education Consortium (http://www.ncrtec.org/), one of ten federally funded regional consortia organized to help K–12 schools implement technology initiatives. UCLA psychologist James W. Stigler, coauthor of the bestselling books *The Teaching Gap* and *The Learning Gap*, founded the LessonLab (http://www.lessonlab.com), a for-profit service that provides a digital library with videos demonstrating instructional techniques and classroom management from places like Japan, Hong Kong, and Switzerland, as well as from high-performing U.S. schools. Its customers include the Los Angeles Unified School District. Another for-profit, TeachFirst (http://www.teachfirst.com), also makes online video a staple of its professional development services.

Schlager says he hopes that the federal government, which has spent millions developing online information clearinghouses such as GEM, ERIC, Eisenhower, and others, will find ways to organize and coordinate those services to maximize their potential as sources of professional sustenance for teachers. "What's needed is not a clearinghouse but a workinghouse," he says. "The emphasis has been on providing content, but not on using the content and adapting it to your practice."

Then there's the nagging question: As foundation and government funding for research projects like Tapped In runs out, can such communities be sustained? For-profit models, such as Classroom Connect, Lesson Lab, and others—all vying for a slice of the $3 billion that K–12 districts will pay this year for professional development—may provide some answers. Or perhaps public-private partnerships like California Learning Interchange will prove to be better models.

Thousands of colleges and universities, professional-development institutes, and for-profit companies have begun offering online courses for teachers. The players range from old, venerable institutions, such as Columbia University's Teachers College, to dot-coms like Connected University, a venture of Harcourt Education Co. As education journalist and researcher Gene I. Maeroff writes in *A Classroom of One*, his 2003 book about online learning: "Purveyors of online learning see elementary and secondary schoolteachers as constituting one of their biggest potential markets. The numbers are huge. About one of every ten undergraduates prepares to teach, and the public and private elementary and secondary schools employ some 3.5 million teachers." High teacher turnover increases the numbers of potential customers of online teacher training, as do collective bargaining agreements and district requirements tying salaries to professional development, Maeroff writes.

It is clear that the demands of No Child Left Behind, which calls for a "highly qualified" teacher in every classroom by the end of the 2005–2006 school year, have created a sense of urgency to develop effective models of staff development. To meet that mandate, teachers will need richer sources of professional sustenance that are easy to access and offered over the course of their school years and their careers, rather than in one-shot seminars on occasional free Fridays. Technology may be one answer to solving at least the logistics of meeting that challenge. As the NCTAF report *No Dream Denied* states, "Technology can provide teachers access to the targeted professional resources they need, when and how they need them. Online courses, informal support groups, and other network supported resources open the door to professional development opportunities far beyond what any school or district might be able to offer."

For Further Information

Corcoran, T. B. (1995). *Transforming professional development for teachers: A guide for policymakers.* Washington, DC: National Governors' Association.

Elmore, R. F. (2002). The limits of change. In M. Pierce & D. L. Stapleton (Eds.), *The 21st-century principal: Current issues in leadership and policy* (pp. 9–18). Cambridge, MA: Harvard Education Press.

Hiebert, J., Gallimore, R., & Stigler, J. W. (2002). A knowledge base for the teaching profession: What would it look like and how can we get one? *Educational Researcher, 31*(5), 3–15.

Johnson, S. M., Birkeland, S., Kardos, S. M., Kauffman, D., Liu, E., & Peske, H. G. (2001). Retaining the next generation of teachers: The importance of school-based support. *Harvard Education Letter, 17*(4), 8, 7.

King, K. P. (2002). Identifying success in online teacher education and professional development. *Internet and Higher Education, 5,* 231–246.

Maeroff, G. I. (2003). *A classroom of one: How online learning is changing our schools and colleges.* New York: Palgrave/St. Martin's.

National Commission on Teaching and America's Future. (2003). *No dream denied: A pledge to America's children.* Washington, DC: Author.

Rodes, P., Knapczyk, D., Chapman, C., & Chung, H. (2000, May). Involving teachers in web-based professional development. *T.H.E. Journal, 27*(10), 95–96, 98, 100, 102.

Smylie, M. A., Allensworth, E., Greenberg, R. C., Harris, R., & Luppescu, S. (2001). *Teacher professional development in Chicago: Supporting effective practice.* Chicago: Consortium on Chicago School Research.

Global Education for Today's World: Creating Hope with Online Learning Communities

By Kristi Rennebohm Franz and Edwin Gragert

Today's world is threaded together by the complex dynamics of global interdependence and dramatic changes in cultural, political, economic, and environmental interconnection across continents. Students' lives are affected by both local and global events. With new technologies, narratives and images of world events near and far are available to students around the world with unprecedented immediacy. As United Nations Secretary-General Kofi Annan (2003) has told U.S. students: "Issues that once seemed very far away are very much in your backyard. What happens in South America or Southern Africa—from democratic advances to deforestation to the fight against AIDS—can affect your lives [here]. And your choices here—what you buy, how you vote—can resound far away. . . . This interdependence generates a host of new and urgent demands."

These demands require the development of international learning communities that connect schools worldwide using new technologies.

Such international collaborations are essential to teaching and learning in this new millennium because they help students to:

1. Understand the complexities of the world—its tapestries of people and places in regional, national, and international contexts

2. Build collaborations between local and global communities, where knowledge across curricular content areas (a) is informed from many perspectives of diversity and commonality across cultures and continents, and (b) prepares students to make constructive contributions in their own communities and with communities worldwide

3. Gain learning experiences, knowledge, and understanding that generate action, support, and hope for a better world

U.S. education leaders recognize the need for international education and are responding with policies that provide for international learning communities using new technologies. In 2000, Education Secretary Richard W. Riley (2000) gave priority to international education as a means of connecting schools worldwide, saying that "[w]e can learn from each other. And we must learn together. We really have no choice. The process of globalization must proceed hand in hand with advances in international education, [or] we will miss the opportunities that the 21st century can offer." In 2002, Riley's successor, Roderick Paige (2002a), reiterated the importance of international education, calling for "programs that introduce our students to international studies earlier in their education, starting in kindergarten."

Teachers also recognize the need to internationalize classroom education. They know that students' views of the world are being defined by what they access on line outside of school and by news coverage about international struggles and conflicts. They know young people are concerned about what tomorrow will bring and see how their students are unsettled by news of disruptive events that endlessly unfold across countries and continents. At the same time, teachers in countries where conflicts are happening know firsthand how such events affect their students' lives, including taking away their opportunity for education. Teachers in all countries want education to improve how students understand and respond to events in their lives, from the local to the global realm.

In schools around the world, teachers share a commitment to have students meet educational standards, pass mandated tests, and prepare to take on the responsibilities of adulthood. Teachers also share a hope that education can empower students to create a better world for themselves, their families, communities, and countries. Many hope that education can build global understanding that leads to peace among people and nations. Their challenge is how to engage students in international learning experiences so today's children and youth can shape their world in positive ways now and in the future.

With new technologies, students and teachers are connecting almost instantly around the globe across time zones, continents, cultures, and languages. The questions for educators become how to use these new technologies most effectively in purposeful international education endeavors and how to do so amidst the array of basic educational experiences we need to provide for our students.

Opportunities for Global Education with New Technologies

Whereas students and teachers used to rely on textbooks to study our world—books often outdated and culturally biased—they now have immediate access to firsthand conversations, experiences, and events happening in the world through new technologies. Students learn needed historical context and current perspectives from authentic voices of peers, teachers, and communities worldwide. They are using Internet technologies to respond to experiences, news, images, and communication of unfolding events that have a global impact. Through direct email, website, and video-conferencing communication with global peers, students collaboratively build understanding of those events. With new technologies, they are finding opportunities to use that knowledge to create a better world.

The K–12 International Education and Resource Network (iEARN) is one example of how educators worldwide conduct local-to-global education with Internet technologies with a view toward improving global understandings (http://www.iearn.org). This international learning community started in 1988, with online communication between students in Russia and the United States, and now includes more than 15,000 schools in 100 countries. More than one million K–12 students are engaged in collaborative school projects worldwide, thereby making meaningful contributions to the health and welfare of people and the planet. Through ID- and password-protected Internet connections, iEARN teachers and students are able to work effectively and economically with one another across continents and among many cultures as they learn critical curricular concepts in connection to events and issues of real-world importance.

Students and their school communities communicate through the iEARN website project forums (http://iearn.org/projects/index.html). Their documented conversations and actions give evidence of progress toward two important educational goals: 1) to build understanding of the interdependent and interconnected dynamics of today's world and 2) to generate opportunities for students to understand how their education can help them take action to meet the challenges facing the world today and tomorrow.

In meeting these two goals, iEARN teachers hope to provide more than just comprehensive curricular content; they also want education to offer hope to students whose lives are affected daily by local, national, and international crises. As Paulo Friere (1992) has stated, "One of the tasks of a progressive educator . . . is to unveil opportunities for hope" (p. 9).

In that spirit, iEARN teachers design curricular projects from a shared educational vision for students to go beyond basic skills to understanding their world from the local to the global realm, and to apply that understanding to shape their world in positive ways. If students can make a difference in their world with what they are learning in school now, they will know they can make a difference after their school years. The iEARN publication *Teacher's Guide to International Collaboration Using the Internet* (2000a) provides examples of how educators can build international communities in their classrooms.

iEARN teachers know that meeting the goals of mandated curricula, standards, and exams can fall short of meeting students' greater needs to understand today's world through education. They share a commitment not to let their goal of internationalizing education be supplanted by short-term local and national education priorities.

Building International Learning Communities in Response to Global Events: Examples from Practice

During the 2000–2001 school year, the international education efforts of the U.S. Department of State and iEARN included exchanges between schools in the United States and the Middle East. In spring 2001, Kristi's school, Sunnyside Elementary, in Pullman, Washington, hosted a teacher from Karachi, Pakistan, for three weeks. Sunnyside students learned about the geographic regions of Pakistan, education in Karachi, and the Urdu language. In return, the students created artwork about caring to give to children in a pediatric hospital in Karachi. Kristi's class created a website of their visit with the Pakistani teacher to share that experience with new school friends in Karachi.

The next fall, when the United States and Pakistan were working together in the aftermath of the attacks of September 11, 2001, Pakistan was not an unfamiliar place to the Sunnyside school community; it had a human face. The importance of the Sunnyside School friendship with Pakistan established prior to September 11 took on even greater significance to this school community. Students had a real-life lesson that building collaborative friendships through education before tragic events occur provides a source of positive connection in the midst of uncertain world events and challenges. This connection between Pakistan and the United States, along with other curricular connections among iEARN schools worldwide, led to the addition of iEARN projects such as BRIDGE (Building Respect through Internet Dialogue and Global Education), which links schools in the United States, the Middle East, North Africa, and South Asia.

In October 2001, the White House and U.S. Department of Education asked iEARN to lead the Friendship through Education (FtE) consortium of Internet education networks (http://www.friendship througheducation.org/) to encourage international collaboration among schools. "Schools Outfitting Schools," one of many FtE initiatives, is a project for students in the United States to provide school supplies to children in Afghanistan, as schools there opened for the first time in years. When Sunnyside Elementary joined this project, Kristi's class used email, digital images, websites, and video production to share their project work with their local community, as an example of how schools could do the project. Their "Schools Outfitting Schools" website and video documentary give evidence of how this project provided curricular learning achievements in literacy, communication, and math while doing international service-learning projects (http://www.iearn.org/afghan/iEARNAfghanistan.html).

In addition to providing school supplies to Afghanistan, schools also have opportunities for sister school partnerships between Afghanistan and the United States. These partnerships are being facilitated by the Afghans for Civil Society, the Harvard University Center for Middle Eastern Studies Outreach Program, and iEARN. The partnerships include email, digital images, and video from Afghanistan documenting the opening of schools there as well as communications sent by U.S. schools to students in Afghanistan. The following poignant email messages sent from Kandahar, Afghanistan, in spring 2003 highlight the value of the partnerships. Ted Achilles of Afghans for Civil Society wrote, "Teachers and students know what it means just to be able to be in school. Nothing is frivolous. Nothing is taken for granted. This is the stuff of life, the future, the hope of a country." A message from an elementary school principal in Kandahar says, "As much as we appreciate receiving supplies, it is really the relationship with the school that means most of all to us."

By communicating with new technologies, students in United States and Afghanistan realize a common shared value of education; they see that together they are shaping their world in positive ways. In Kandahar, the hope of access to education, which for so long was suspended, has become a reality with support from U.S. schools. In the United States, students, teachers, and families have a new appreciation for what it means to get to attend school each day as they learn how important education is to students and teachers in Afghanistan.

Since 1994, Kristi's classroom of primary students has collaborated with schools on five continents in online curricular projects that integrate science, social studies, world languages, math, literacy, visual arts, and service learning. As part of an integrated literacy, communication, and new technologies curriculum, Kristi's students learn to write about their global learning projects on the classroom website (http://www.psd267.wednet.edu/~kfranz). Through global communication, they have gained important understanding of the world and learned how to take positive action with what they learned, while meeting educational goals and standards (Rennebohm Franz, 2001). Their iEARN water habitat project exemplifies this and is documented as a "Picture of Practice" on the Harvard Graduate School of Education Teaching for Understanding website (http://learnweb.harvard.edu/ent/home/index.cfm) (Rennebohm Franz, 2000a). As these young students connect on line from rural eastern Washington, they assume that new technologies are a way to learn in school. School is a place where they know first-hand that what they learn in their classroom and community has connections to the world as a whole. They know, from their first years in school, that they can make a difference in the world through their education.

For videos of Kristi's classroom that illustrate the effects on classroom curricula of international collaborations using new technologies, see the North Central Regional Education Laboratory (NCREL) enGauge website addresses listed in the references at the end of this article. The George Lucas Education Foundation (GLEF) also documents examples of how educators and students are using the Internet and other multimedia tools to build social contexts for global understanding (http://glef.org/edutopiaarc.html). GLEF executive director Milton Chen says about the importance of using new technologies to build international learning communities: "The World Wide Web is leading a new generation of World Wide Thinkers—students who understand that the world and their own learning have no borders" (George Lucas Educational Foundation, 2002, p. 2).

Before the development of these new technologies, international school partnerships were built almost entirely through exchange programs. Fortunately, opportunities for students to learn firsthand from one another's voices and experiences are no longer limited to who can physically travel the geographic distance of the world. With the click of the mouse or a few keystrokes, the world is now in the hands of students worldwide.

A Philosophical Framework for International Learning Communities

The following principles, first identified in the context of creating a framework for developing a critical social consciousness through local-to-global education (Rennebohm Franz, 1996), can guide international K–12 collaborations. They have emerged from the dynamics and experiences of teachers and students participating in iEARN curricular projects, which have shown that respect and inclusion of one another's ideas and perspectives are essential for building positive global education collaborations.

1. Students' experiences in their own community have a connection to the experiences of students worldwide. These connections may include geographic locations, habitats, natural and human-made resources, cultures, languages, friendships, families, work, responsibilities, and accomplishments, as well as hopes, concerns, and challenges.
2. The commonalities that students discover among one another across cultures and continents affirm how alike people are; their diversities offer opportunities for understanding people and places in ways not previously imagined.

3. Learning with peers globally is not a competitive endeavor but a collaborative process that invites the constructive participation of many. Collaboration is based on recognizing that today's world is a complex system of people and places where many voices are needed to comprehend the whole. Participation in global collaborations is not a pathway to being first in the world but a process of building a better world for all.

4. Differing perspectives and experiences can have validity and reciprocal value without the expectation that, because views are different, one side must be right and the other wrong.

5. Learning includes an ongoing revision of knowledge as new sources of information become available, new discoveries emerge, and new opportunities unfold for dialogue and collaboration with global reach, participation, and contribution.

6. As students collaborate in International Learning Communities, they can envision ways to take collaborative actions with their new understanding that generate reciprocal respect and benefit among people in places around the world.

It is critically important to build cultures of respect within global communities of teaching and learning. Sara Lawrence-Lightfoot (2002) offers a "new view of respect" focusing on "the way respect creates symmetry, empathy, and connection in all kinds of relationships." Her view of respect has relevance to students developing collaborations with one another to improve global understanding. She writes:

> Rather than look for respect as a given in certain relationships, I am interested in watching it develop over time. I see it not only as an expression of circumstance, history, temperament, and culture rooted in rituals and beliefs, but also arising from efforts to

break routine and imagine other ways of giving and receiving trust, and in so doing, creating relationships among equals. (p. 10)

Students learn best when they have the opportunities and mentoring to build respectful international communities of shared understanding and support for one another. They develop leadership abilities in global problem-solving when they have opportunities to respectfully share collective wisdom, questions, skills, and resources in response to human needs and resolution of conflicts. In the words of Daniel Reyes, one of the founders of iEARN from Argentina, "There is no one without something to teach. There is no one so endowed that he/she has nothing to learn from the other" (Gragert, 2003).

It is clear that new technologies have made international learning communities possible. But in building such communities, educators need to focus less on the technologies and more on the human interactions they enable. For the power of the Internet to be fully utilized, it must be more than a huge library. Its real power is in how the online human interactions bring about changes in attitudes, understanding, and actions. As Edwin Gragert (2002) writes:

As we are able to connect instantly from the simplest text-based email connection to a full range of multi-media interactive tools, it still will come down to "listening and hearing" if we are truly to use this amazing technology for an educational purpose; it is a process of active learning with and from one another that prepares us as learners and citizens of the planet to exponentially connect across cultures with respect and understanding.

As students learn about and understand the challenges of the world today, they want to take action with what they know. Education is no longer an end in itself, but rather a pathway to shaping a better world. In many classrooms around the world, where students are using new technologies to learn about and contribute to their local and global communities, there is a seamless connection between getting an education and making positive differences with that education.

From kindergarten through high school, international education collaborations with new technologies are defining social contexts for learning in the 21st century. New technologies provide opportunities for students to realize that what they learn in the social context of global collaborations extends their understanding of curricular content and of the wider world. Teachers think of their students' email and website communication as an online version of Vygotskian verbal communication tools for social thinking to develop conceptual understandings (Vygotsky, 1978). Indeed, international learning communities give opportunities for what Vygotsky calls "learning as a profoundly social process," which "emphasizes dialogue and the varied roles language plays in instruction and in mediated cognitive growth" (p. 131).

Professional Development for International Collaboration

To support online international education efforts, teacher professional development is essential. In the initial stages of connecting globally, we suggest that schools join active online projects led by educators with experiences in facilitating global curricular teaching and learning with new technologies. This provides opportunities for teachers to learn from their peers as they and their students begin international learning community participation, without the added responsibility of designing a project. It is helpful if teachers join existing projects that have connections to their current classroom curricula. For example, if a water habitat project is already part of a classroom, the teacher may choose to have students contribute their habitat science work on line to share with other schools doing a similar study. All schools need not follow the same process of assignments or learning tasks. Although curricula vary considerably around the world, teachers can communicate online to identify commonalities of topics and concepts, which can be helpful in planning joint projects.

Teachers and students have often found that, as they communicate globally, they learn new ideas for teaching and learning, which they then integrate locally. iEARN online professional development courses (http://iearn.org/professional/index.html) dramatically reduce the learning curve for teachers who want to integrate international collaborative project learning into their classrooms. Another online resource is *iEARN Connecting Cultures: A Teacher's Guide to a Global Classroom* (iEARN, 2000b).

As teachers start to integrate international learning collaborations into their classrooms, these online opportunities open up numerous possibilities for student learning, often beyond what teachers had anticipated and beyond the scope of local district curricula. Curricular topics become generative as students work together; as students do online inquiry, new understanding emerges, leading to new directions for teaching and learning. Students often demonstrate performances beyond original learning goals. As teachers try to articulate and organize the experiences of international learning communities, they often need to redesign their curricula to reflect those experiences.

One particularly useful conceptual process for designing such curricula is Teaching for Understanding (TfU), developed at the Harvard Graduate School of Education. TfU's components—Generative Topics, Understanding Goals, Performances of Understanding, Ongoing Assessment and Community (Wiske, 1998, 2003)—provide a conceptual process for designing curricula for local teaching and learning. For example, Performances of Understanding include criteria for identifying and planning learning experiences that go beyond introductory information to guided inquiry and culminating performances. These criteria are an excellent match for learning in which students apply what they learn in global collaboration to make positive contributions in local and global communities. The TfU Education with New Technologies website (http://learnweb.harvard.edu/ent/home/index.cfm) includes a Collaborative Curricular Design Tool for teachers across countries and continents to work together globally on their shared curricula. Educators can also take online courses to learn about and use TfU pedagogy (http://wideworld.pz.harvard.edu/eng/home/index.cfm).

Making the Commitment to Online Global Education

As students' lives are influenced by global events, education that connects them to the world is essential. Online learning communities enable them to understand and have hope for their world today amidst the tensions and realities of unfolding international events. Student global collaborations, such as project learning in the iEARN community, demonstrate that children and youth can contribute to making a better world when learning with global peers. Teachers, parents, and communities are inspired by what students accomplish in the collaborations and see how the collaborations prepare them for taking responsibility for their world.

As students use technology to build a new understanding of the world, they are experiencing education differently than their parents and many of their teachers did when they were in school. Their online collaborations enable them to develop positive construction of knowledge of the world with global peers. From community to community, region to region, and across the continents, students and teachers can and do weave global tapestries of education that make a difference in the world.

In today's classrooms, providing hope for global peace is one of the major challenges of education. It is a challenge that must be met. As former U.S. President Jimmy Carter said when accepting the Nobel Peace Prize, "People everywhere share the same dream of a caring international community that prevents war and oppression. . . . We can choose to work together for peace. We can—and we must" (Carter, 2002, p. 20). Supporting online international learning communities is one way we can help meet that challenge.

References and Other Resources

Afghans for Civil Society [Website]. (2003). Available online at http://www.afghansforcivilsociety.org/

Annan, K. (2003). *Commencement address at Duke University*. Available online at http://www.dukenews.duke.ed/news/

Carter, J. (2002). *The Nobel Peace Prize lecture*. New York: Simon & Schuster.

Vygotsky, L. S. (1978). *Mind in society: The development of higher psychological processes* (M. Cole, V. John-Steiner, S. Schribner, & E. Souberman, Editors). Cambridge, MA: Harvard University Press.

Einhorn, C., Frederick, B., Gragert, E., Meirhoefer, B., Rennebohm Franz, K., & Vilela, A. (1997a). *It takes many villages to build a world: Honoring people and learning* (Teacher Internet Professional Development Three Day Module for the World Bank World Links for Development Program [WorLD]). Available online at http://www.iearn.org/world

Freire, P. (1992). *Pedagogy of hope*. New York: Continuum.

George Lucas Educational Foundation. (2002, Spring). *Edutopia*, p. 2. Available online at http://glef.org/edutopiaarc.html

Gragert, E. (2002, July 12). *Learning from the other*. Available online at http://www.learningchannel.org/article/view/60010/1/

Gragert, E. (2003). The Internet + laws of life = 54 countries writing, sharing and learning. *Laws of Life Contest* [newsletter]. Available online at http://www.lawsoflife.org/pdf/lolnewsletters/2003_Winter.PDF

Harvard University Graduate School of Education WIDE World Online Professional Development for Teachers and Educators [Website]. (2003). Available online at http://wideworld.pz.harvard.edu/eng/home/index.cfm

Harvard University Graduate School of Education Teaching for Understanding Education with New Technologies [Website]. (2003). Available online at http://learnweb.harvard.edu/ent/home/index.cfm

International Education and Resource Network. (2000a). *Teacher's guide to international collaboration using the Internet*. Washington, DC: U.S. Department of Education. Available online at http://www.ed.gov/Technology/guide/international/index.html

International Education and Resource Network. (2000b). *iEARN connecting cultures: A teacher's guide to a global classroom*. Available online at http://iearn.org/professional/index.html

International Education and Resource Network [Website]. (2003). Available online at http://www.iearn.org

Lawrence-Lightfoot, S. (2002). *Respect: An exploration*. Cambridge, MA: Perseus.

Paige, R. (2002a, November 30). *Comments to the States Institute on International Education*. Washington, DC: U.S. Department of Education. Available online at http://www.ed.gov/Speeches/11-2002/11202002.html

Paige, R. (2002b, November). *Comments to Friendship through Education Consortium Reception*. Available online at http://www. friendshipthrougheducation.org/paige.html

Rennebohm Franz, K. (1996). Toward a critical social consciousness in children: Multicultural peace education in a first grade classroom. *Theory Into Practice, 35*, 264–270.

Rennebohm Franz, K. (2000a). *Teaching for Understanding, a picture of practice: iEARN water habitat project.* Available online at http://learnweb. harvard.edu/ent/gallery/pop3/pop3_1.cfm

Rennebohm Franz, K. (2000b). *The pedagogical practice behind the technology in a primary classroom.* enGauge [Website]. Available online at http:// www.ncrel.org/engauge/framewk/efp/research/efpressu.htm

Rennebohm Franz, K. (2000c). *Literacy learning through technology: Primary classroom.* enGauge [Website]. Available online at http://www.ncrel. org/ engauge/framewk/efp/environ/efpenvsu.htm

Rennebohm Franz, K. (2000d). *There's a lot of learning going on—Use multiple assessments to capture IT all.* enGauge [Website]. Available online at http:// www.ncrel.org/engauge/framewk/efp/align/efpalisu.htm

Rennebohm Franz, K. (2001). Improving education. In *Connecting cultures: A teacher's guide to a global classroom.* Available online at http://www.iearn. org/professional/index.html

Rennebohm Franz, K. (2003a). Sunnyside Elementary School Classroom [Website]. Available online at http://www.psd267.wednet.edu/~kfranz

Rennebohm Franz, K. (2003b). *Building a world through education: Launching essential learnings from Washington state USA to Afghanistan* (iEARN and Afghans for Civil Society Partnership). Available online at http://www.iearn. org/afghan/iEARNAfghanistan.html

Riley, R. W. (2000, May 30). *Remarks by Secretary of Education Richard W. Riley at the American Chamber of Commerce, Milan, Italy.* Washington, DC: U.S. Department of Education. Available online at http://www.ed.gov/offices/ OUS/PES/discussion_paper.html

States Institute on International Education in the Schools [Website]. (2002). Available online at http://www.asiaintheschools.org/states.htm

Washington State International Education Coalition. (2003). *Strategic intent statement.* Available online at http://internationaledwa.org/summit/flyernotes. htm

Wiske, M. S. (Ed.). (1998). *Teaching for understanding: Linking research with practice*. San Francisco: Jossey-Bass.

Wiske, M. S. (with Rennebohm Franz, K., & Breit, L.). (2003). *Teaching for understanding with new technologies*. San Francisco: Jossey-Bass.

For Further Information: A Web Sampler

There are literally thousands of websites devoted to education, and each may have hundreds of pages buried within them. Sorting out the helpful from the useless can be not only difficult but time consuming. But that shouldn't discourage educators from using these incredible resources. Instead they need to learn how to assess and exploit them, if for no other reason than to teach their students how to do so, for that is one of the primary skills 21st-century learners must have. What follows is a sampling of websites that offer helpful resources to K–12 professionals, parents, and students.

AllYouCanRead.com
http://www.allyoucanread.com/newspapers.asp
Neatly organized links to newspapers and magazines from all over the world, from China's *People's Liberation Army Daily* to *El Tiempo* in Peru to Michigan's *Kalamazoo Gazette*. Includes a "Country of the Week" profile.

ArtsEdge
http://artsedge.kennedy-center.org/
Sponsored by the John F. Kennedy Center for the Performing Arts in Washington, D.C., ArtsEdge offers a number of "mini-sites," described as "multidisciplinary, self-contained explorations of arts-related themes or subjects." Nested in these pages are instructional activities, multimedia fea-

tures, and primary sources on topics such as the Harlem Renaissance, Irish culture, and Asian art, as well as biographical lessons about Louis Armstrong, Marian Anderson, and others. It also provides a place for teachers to exchange lessons, activities, web links, and more.

AskERIC

http://www.askeric.org
Drawing on the 16 clearinghouses of the Educational Resources Information Center (ERIC) system, this "superportal" offers links, lesson plans, a searchable database, and a Q&A service to teachers, librarians, counselors, administrators, and parents. Literally thousands of helpful, research-based resources are available here with a few keystrokes.

Busy Teachers' Website K–12

http://www.ceismc.gatech.edu/busyt/
With a clean, easy-to-use layout, this site links teachers to lesson plans, classroom activities, and other resources, including connections to online teacher-to-teacher discussion groups and e-journals. Organized by subject.

Eisenhower National Clearinghouse for Mathematics and Science Education

http://www.enc.org
Teachers visiting this site will find a large, searchable database of K–12 math and science curriculum resources, as well as professional development tools and helpful articles about education research and practice. Assessment, technology implementation, and real-world math and science projects are also featured. Topics are well organized by subject.

EDSitement

http://edsitement.neh.gov/
A rich resource for humanities instruction at all levels. Includes lesson plans and links for arts and culture, foreign languages, literature and language arts, and history and social studies. Organized by subject matter, it includes indications of how lessons meet various standards.

Edutopia Online
http://www.glef.org
The nonprofit George Lucas Educational Foundation, organized by the creator of the *Star Wars* and *Indiana Jones* movies, is a superb multimedia resource for anyone with a stake in improving K–12 schools. Magazine-style articles, slideshows, and a video gallery demonstrate innovative classroom practices, professional development, parent involvement, and school-business partnerships. The video gallery includes more than 70 interviews with school leaders, researchers, and teachers, as well as 50 original documentary films.

Gateway to Educational Materials (GEM)
http://www.thegateway.org
This huge, searchable megasite sponsored by the U.S. Department of Education offers educators quick and easy access to thousands of educational resources found on various federal, state, university, nonprofit, and commercial Internet sites, as well as public school sites.

Global Schoolhouse
http://www.globalschoolhouse.org/
A clearinghouse of hundreds of online collaborative learning projects, web resources, and stories of extraordinary teachers. Includes tutorials on how to develop online collaborative learning projects, a place for students to write and post online newspapers, and much more.

Gloria's Writing Workshop
www3.sk.sympatico.ca/fiss
For classroom teachers who want to use a workshop approach to writing instruction, this site offers a plan for teaching the stages of writing, holding conferences to discuss work with student writers, and more.

Harvard Education Letter
http://www.edletter.org
You'll find articles by leading researchers, K–12 practitioners, and education journalists about the latest in education research and classroom-tested teaching strategies.

History Matters
http://historymatters.gmu.edu/
A rich, innovative site made for teachers of U.S. history, History Matters tells the good, the bad, the beautiful, and the ugly of the past 200 years, with a special emphasis on social history. Lesson plans, links, references, and tips from master history teachers are all part of the package.

iEARN
http://www.iearn.org
This nonprofit network facilitates the creation of project-based collaborations among schools from all over the globe as a way of providing students with tools for international understanding, cooperation, and conflict resolution.

Internet Public Library's Ask Author
http://www.ipl.org/youth/AskAuthor/
Sponsored by the University of Michigan, this site includes an incredible list of resources for educators and students. "KidSpace" and "TeenSpace" sections are specially designed for students with links to helpful resources and pages.

Kathy Schrock's Guide for Educators
http://school.discovery.com/schrockguide
This comprehensive resource, produced by a school technology specialist, lists a wealth of websites for enhancing classroom teaching and learning, as well as professional development. Identifies links that are particularly content-rich.

Library of Congress
http://www.loc.gov
A superior resource, this site offers an incredible array of resources, including video and audio, photographs, original documents, maps, timelines, and more. Special collections include American Memory, which archives more than seven million documents related to U.S. history and culture, and Global Gateway, a similar service focused on international themes. These teacher-friendly pages have lesson plans and activities, and teachers can apply to take part in summer workshops at the Library of Congress in Washington, D.C., to learn how to better use these extraordinary resources.

Lives
http://amillionlives.com/
A portal to biographical websites, listed both by individual (alphabetically) and by groupings. The latter are organized by historical era, profession, race, geographical location, events, etc. Also provides resources on biographical criticism and special collections.

Math Forum
http://www.mathforum.org/
For K–12 teachers who wish to "Ask Dr. Math" questions about instruction and curriculum, peruse a library of lesson plans, challenge themselves to solve tricky math problems, or join web-based conversations with other educators, this well-organized, pioneering site is the place to go.

MiddleWeb
http://www.middleweb.com
This colorful site deals with all things "middle school." In addition to curriculum resources, it offers links to articles in mainstream and education press about middle schools, teacher diaries, and listservs where teachers connect to talk about their practice.

NASA Quest Archives
http://quest.arc.nasa.gov/hst/index.html
Space exploration continues to be a source of discovery and fascination for students of all ages. This site provides lesson plans and student activities for all grade levels, links to science and technology standards, a searchable Q&A section, and audiovisual resources, as well as inspiring biographies of astronauts and explanations of what they do.

National Center for Research on Evaluations, Standards, and Student Testing (CRESST)
http://cresst96.cse.ucla.edu
This research-focused website offers a range of helpful reports on policy and practice, a glossary, a "Parent's Page," and even a Q&A service, through which you can email CRESST experts for answers to your questions about assessments, high-stakes testing, and more. Especially helpful in light of the federal No Child Left Behind Act.

New York Times Learning Network
http://www.nytimes.com/learning/
This terrific resource for K–12 teachers, students, and parents offers a variety of lesson plans, including activities related to current news events. Also provides links to other educational sites, organized by curricular subject.

Refdesk.com
http://www.refdesk.com
This encyclopedic portal collects links to literally hundreds of helpful sites, including reference books, directories, almanacs, and more.

Story Place
http://www.storyplace.org/
Created by public librarians and targeted at a K–5 audience, this colorful site offers reading lists as well as reading-related games and other activities. Students get to post their own stories, too.

TappedIn

http://www.tappedin.org

This is an online, international "workplace" for K–12 professionals, where teacher education faculty and students, researchers, and others committed to improving schools can take part in professional development programs and informal collaboration with colleagues. Membership is free, and teachers can set up their own online offices where they can confer privately or in groups with colleagues, post lesson plans or articles they've written, and exchange ideas. A fun, informative place to visit.

techs4schools

http://techs4schools.techcorps.org/

Information technology experts from companies like Hewlitt Packard and Cisco offer their time and expertise to help school practitioners take advantage of the power of new technologies. Teachers can sign up for an online mentor who will answer technical questions about everything from getting a printer to work to using Microsoft products on an Appleshare system.

WebQuest

http://webquest.sdsu.edu/

For inquiry- or problem-based projects, check out this website developed at San Diego State University. A good site for teaching students not only how to find information on the Web but also how to evaluate and use that information in practical ways.

webTeacher

http://www.webteacher.org/

Created by two teachers and volunteers from TECHCORPS, a nonprofit support service for teachers, webTeacher offers training tools and tutorials to help teachers use the Internet, email, videoconferencing, and other new technologies. Not sure what is meant by animated gif, screen captures, and background tiling? Then this is the site for you. Includes a Spanish translation.

Notes on Contributors

David T. Gordon is editor of the award-winning *Harvard Education Letter*, a bimonthly publication about K–12 education research and practice written in a jargon-free way for school administrators, teachers, parents, and policymakers. He has edited the books *A Nation Reformed? American Education 20 Years After* A Nation at Risk (2003) and *The Digital Classroom: How Technology Is Changing the Way We Teach and Learn* (2000). Before coming to Harvard in 1999, he was an associate editor at *Newsweek*, where he wrote about education, foreign affairs, culture, and technology. He is the recipient of the 2003 National Press Club Award for best newsletter journalism.

Edwin Gragert is executive director of iEARN-USA (International Education and Resource Network), which has pioneered the use of telecommunications technology to facilitate online educational project work at the primary and secondary school level. His articles on international collaborative learning through online technologies have appeared in numerous educational technology publications and journals. Dr. Gragert provides leadership on international education in the United States and to school communities and ministries of education worldwide. He received a degree in Japanese political science from the University of Washington–Seattle, as well as an M.A. in Korean history and a Ph. D. in Japanese history from Columbia University. His book, *Landownership under Colonial Rule: Korea's Japa-*

nese Experience, was published jointly by Columbia University Press and the University of Hawaii Press in 1994.

James Moore is an instructional designer working with web-based environments to support teaching and learning. He teaches instructional design at the Harvard Graduate School of Education. Dr. Moore's recent work focuses on the development of online communities to support the mentoring of new teachers.

David Niguidula is a researcher in educational technology, and consults with schools and districts through his firm, Ideas Consulting. Dr. Niguidula led the original research on digital portfolios while managing the technology group for the Coalition of Essential Schools and Annenberg Institute for School Reform at Brown University. He has worked with schools and districts throughout the U.S. and overseas. He has also taught or co-taught classes in the computer science department at Brown and at Teachers College, Columbia University.

Cathleen A. Norris is a professor in the Department of Technology and Cognition at the University of North Texas College of Education in Denton. Her efforts in research, teaching, and service all have a common focus: to integrate learning technologies more effectively into K–12 and postsecondary classrooms. In the Snapshotsurvey Project, Dr. Norris is surveying educators around the country to better understand their uses of, beliefs about, and needs for technology in the classroom (http://snapshotsurvey.org). Through her WebKids Project, she explores design guidelines that address the unique needs of children, and with her FindResearch Project, Dr. Norris is developing strategies to help educators extract value from the research literature on technology in education.

Andrea Oseas is executive director of the Center on Media and Child Health at Children's Hospital and the Harvard School of Public Health. She was previously assistant director of the Technology in Education Program and an instructor at the Harvard Graduate School of Education. She is also a painter.

Kristi Rennebohm Franz is a teacher with expertise in implementing international learning communities in classroom curricula. She has taught at the International School of Kenya, Sunnyside Elementary in Pullman, Washington, and is a lead teacher for the International Education and Resource Network (iEARN), as well as a member of its U.S. board of directors. She has held visiting appointments at the Harvard University Graduate School of Education to collaborate on new technologies in education. She is on the editorial board of *Education, Communication, and Information.* Her classroom teaching was featured in the PBS documentary *Digital Divide,* and she is the recipient of the first Paul D. Coverdell World Wise Schools Peace Corps Award for Excellence in Education, the Presidential Award for Excellence in Science Teaching, and the Milken National Educator Award.

Michael Sadowski is the assistant editor of the *Harvard Education Letter* and the editor of *Adolescents at School: Perspectives on Youth, Identity, and Education* (Harvard Education Press, 2003). A former high school teacher, he is an instructor and an advanced doctoral candidate at the Harvard Graduate School of Education.

Elliot Soloway is a professor in the College of Engineering, the School of Education, and the School of Information at the University of Michigan. For the past 14 years, Dr. Soloway and his colleagues at the Center for Highly Interactive Computing in Education (HI-CE) have explored the ways computing and communications technologies can be the catalyst for bringing a constructivist, inquiry-based pedagogy to K–12 science classrooms.

Julie M. Wood is an educational consultant, speaker, and writer. She is a former director of the Jeanne Chall Reading Laboratory at the Harvard Graduate School of Education, where she also served as a faculty member in the Technology in Education Program. Dr. Wood's book *Cyberkids: Struggling Readers and Writers and How Computers Can Help* (working title) is scheduled to be published by Heinemann in 2004.

Louise Grace Yarnall is a research social scientist at SRI International in Menlo Park, California, where her work includes exploring ways to use new technologies to support richer learning for students challenged by environmental, cultural, physical, or neurological limitations. Her commitment to providing accessible information to a wide audience began through her initial 10-year career as newspaper reporter whose work appeared in the *Los Angeles Times* and *New York Times*. The birth of her two sons inspired a professional shift toward research into education, and Yarnall earned her doctorate in 2002 from UCLA's Graduate School of Education and Information Studies.